Win
On Purpose

Finding a Better Way
and Sharing It!

Jerry M. Lujan

Table of Contents

Forward *by Kelley Lujan*

Introduction   5

Why Don't You Love Me?   16

Something Had to Change   23

It Played Out Like Reality TV   27

Had I Actually Worked the Best Years of My Life Away?   31

*What the C.R.A.P. is Happening in the Insurance Sales
Business?*   36

The Danger of Commodity Thinking   52

It's Hard to Hit a Roving Target   59

*What the C.R.A.P.? The Agency Death Spiral: What You
Can Do To Stop It?*   71

What the C.R.A.P? The Professional Agent   84

The BGRAT System: Balance   99

It's Déjà vu All Over Again: Goals   110

Relationships and Opportunities   121

Attitude and Gratitude   131

Tools, Coaches and Mentors, Oh My! The Essentials   149

Conclusion   158

Forward

By Kelley Lujan

     As I think back, and remember the time I spent with my dad, two prominent things come to mind: business and baseball. Virtually every family outing or conversation we had revolved around one of those two subjects. From those two topics, my dad instilled in me the core values that I would need to be successful, not only in school and business, but in life as well. I learned that in order to be great at something, I have to practice. The top experts in the world would not be where they are today without tireless hours of practice. He also taught me that I can not be perfect. Whenever I am struggling with something, he always reminds me that it is the progress that counts, not the perfection. My daddy had 5 golden rules when we were growing up, which he learned from his coach, Dan Sullivan, and passed onto us.

1. Show up on time.
2. Do what you say.
3. Finish what you start.
4. Say please and thank you.
5. Treat others how you want to be treated.

I have found these to hold true in every aspect of my life.

Ever since I was a young girl, my daddy taught me that I could do anything that I set my mind to. My dad was the business mind in the family. Anytime that my brother or I needed advice for the future or on a certain project, my dad would be the first person we would go to. He was one of the most successful, business oriented people that I knew. Whatever project I was working on, he would always encourage me to make it the best I could because he knew what I was truly capable of and believed in me.

I remember when I was little, every time that I would have an idea or something that I wanted to do, I had to make a presentation for my Dad regarding what I wanted to do, why it was important, and some of the logistics behind it. Every time I would make one of these presentations, I always knew I was on to something when I could see his eyes light up and that huge smile come across his face. He could recognize when I was passionate about something. I knew that when he recognized that passion, he would do anything in the world to support me. For example, when I was little my dad made a promise to me that if I worked hard enough and got the grades that I needed to get into any university of my choice, that he would make it happen, no matter the cost.

As I grew older, my Daddy and I were able to continue to share this unique bond. He has presented me with so many opportunities for growth. He has also taught me to cherish these opportunities. I have had the opportunity to meet extremely influential people and mentors in the business world that have taught me and inspired me to achieve much of what I have today.

Four years ago my Daddy kept that promise that we made when I was younger. Today, I am a graduating senior from the University of San Diego. Now more than ever, my Dad's support for me and my life goals have shined through. I have learned that school, work, and life all revolve around the relationships you form.

Introduction

I am at war with mediocrity.

And I'm using all the weapons in my arsenal to destroy it forever. I'm also enlisting those like-minded individuals – in whatever industry they may work – to join me in my army.

I'm thrilled that you're considering joining me in my fight against complacency and the ordinary. If you feel the same way – and want to start by improving your own performance, then you've come to the right place!

Not only am I at war with mediocrity, but I love helping winners. I love taking those who sincerely want to get ahead in life and do exactly this. I get a real kick out of seeing them climb to the top of their chosen fields. The combination of these two desires has come together in me so that I couldn't help but write this book.

It was as if it had been forming, germinating for years inside of me before it was ready to spring forth in this manner in order to spread the exciting words of success.

I'd love nothing better than to lay out the entire feast of life before you right now in this single paragraph, but it's the story that holds this feast and I'm eager for you to begin this very moment on improving your performance and your professional and personal relationships.

As we take this journey together, you'll understand – from listening to some of the stories I tell inspired by my own career and personal life – exactly why I view this not as a job, or a favor to you, but as my life's mission to find a better way and share it. Just stay with me! I promise you the ride of a lifetime.

I can also tell you're a responsible professional. As we trek through the chapters, seeking out and destroying mediocrity – you'll see exactly what I mean. True professionals, for one thing, always know there's room for improvement. They never rest on their laurels.

Why I Wrote This Book

I've written this book for two reasons. First, because I wandered in the wilderness for 20 years, working hard to get to the top of the sales industry. In the process, I came so close to destroying my health. I was putting in a minimum of 60 hours a week, trying to top the business I had brought in the year before . . . the month before . . . the week before – even the day before.

I never took a vacation. Heck, I never even took the time to spend days with my family. As you can probably already surmise, my family life wasn't healthy either. By anyone's standards I appeared successful – except the standards I had set for myself and the expectations of my family.

It took the simple question of my then, five-year-old daughter to finally knock some sense into me. That's when I took a good, long look at what caused me to do this, to push myself to the brink of destruction in so many ways.

The Sales Industry and The C.R.A.P. I Tolerated

I lived and breathed the sales industry. I thought by doing this I would eventually find exactly what I had been looking for – wild monetary success. And in that area I did. But I overlooked something very important.

I had assumed that after I reached a certain pinnacle in the career, I could slow down some. Then when I slowed down, I told myself, I could then enjoy the company of my family. There was a slight snag in my thinking. What was that?

I didn't count on the fact that once I did hit that pinnacle that I needed to keep on plugging away. In fact, I needed to work even harder at that point, in order to keep what I've already earned. I had pushed my family to the brink during the past 20 years only to discover that I still wasn't going to have the time I thought I would to spend with them.

By this time, I had thought a few things through. Among them were the cold, hard facts that the sales industry was riddled with what I called, "Five Fatal Flaws." These are the problems that most people in the sales industry knew existed, but failed to address.

I refer to these flaws by an acronym I created: The C.R.A.P. As you can tell, I hold just a bit of disdain toward these problems deeply embedded in the fabric of the insurance sales industry or most any sales industry, for that matter. The term stands for:

The – Trust

C   -- Commodity

R   -- Roving targets

A   -- Agency Death Spiral

P   -- Professionalism.

I'll tell you how I was able to rise above mediocrity by eliminating these fatal flaws. In doing so, I was able to create a thriving career that was less dependent on the number of hours I put into it and more on the relationships I made.

You'll be interested in learning more about these lessons. You, no doubt, will recognize some, if not all, of them. And you'll gain insight learning how I handled these circumstances.

The Five Fundamental Filters

In addition to learning about the five fatal flaws of the industry, I also talk (in the last half of the book) about what I call filters. These are essentially using these guideposts to help me cope, organize and, yes, thrive in the industry.

In the first section of this book, you'll see my picture (perspective) of the industry. The long, grueling hours a professional must work, the humility he must subject himself to because his customers think of him and his products as commodities — not services and results — as the limitations inherent in all of this.

Then, We Reach The Second Half of Our Journey

Please, stay with me for the second section. In this section, we really dig deep to solve the growing problem of mediocrity. I show you how you can overcome the misconceptions of your customers, the failures of the industry to provide you the respect you rightly deserve and, most importantly of all, how to make an amazing living and still win the love and respect of your family or whatever it is that you love most in your life.

Sound too good to be true? Remember, you agreed to enlist in my fight against mediocrity because you know, deep in your heart, there's a better, more professional, more profitable and, yes, more humane way of conducting business and succeeding. All without sacrificing your health or the love of your family.

The tricks I'll teach you in this section I like to call "BGRAT." In this section, you're essentially learning how to control the odds. I'll teach you how to take those odds and work them to play in your favor.

If you've ever been to Las Vegas or Atlantic City you know the moment you enter a casino, the odds are stacked in the house's favor. That's part of the thrill of gambling – trying to be that person who beat the house odds.

Of course, it's a little less spectacular when you find yourself fighting for your own prosperity. Given enough time, you may even come to resent that the house, in this case the insurance industry, holds the odds.

Trust me, though. You'll discover how, using these simple principles, you can beat the house at its own game.

The system I use doesn't have such a grand name as The C.R.A.P. – what I've named the flaws. But if you can remember these initials: B.G.R.A.T. then you'll never doubt your chances of success again.

What exactly does B.G.R.A.T. stand for?

B – Balance

G – Goals

R – Relationships

A – Attitude and Gratitude

T – Tools, Coaches and Mentors

When you use these you'll discover that success is just around the corner. I'll tell you exactly what happens when I'm using these filters to guide my practices. It'll give you some idea of how you'll benefit from them. When I consciously use these, then I'm confident I'm working at my full potential. These are the guidelines that I've used to provide me not only professional success, but personal satisfaction as well.

When I'm using these in a purposeful, dedicated manner, I receive outstanding results. No exceptions. The results I find are far better than I anything I can do by dancing around them. I believe they're so important in my life, that I have them posted on my wall as a daily reminder of how they've transformed my life.

Yes, despite how amazed I am with their productive results, there were those moments when I allowed my eyes to stray from these filters. And when I have, I have floundered both personally and professionally.

Are you ready to transform your life from mediocrity to excellence? There's no time like the present to start!

Chapter 1

Why Don't You Love Me?

She met me at the door that day, her hands on her hips, her toes tapping the floor. "I've been waiting for you," she said, looking up at me. I thought it was an unusual stance for a five year old, but then again, she had been precocious since the day she was born. At least that's what I liked to tell people.

I bent down and gave her a kiss. She usually gave me a hug. She didn't this time. Kelley continued to stand there. Kelley is my daughter and when I look into those big black eyes, I can't help but see my wife, Lisa. This little girl is well on her way to growing up to being an amazing young lady. It is evident even at this young of an age.

On this particular day, though, she looked exceedingly serious. Far too serious for being so young.

"It looks as if you have a specific reason for waiting for me, sweetheart," I said, as I sidestepped her to enter the living room.

"I do," she replied as she followed me. I placed my briefcase down and then sat on the couch. I invited her to sit next to me.

"No, thank you," she said formally. "I'll sit here." And she climbed up on a chair not far from the couch. If any adult could be in the doghouse with a five year old, I thought that at the very moment I was.

She wasted no time and minced no words in telling me what she wanted. "I want to make an appointment to go to the park with you," she announced, her face still as stern as the moment I stepped in the house.

My initial reaction was one of amusement. *What an observant little girl,* I thought. She had heard her mother and me talking about my insurance sales business and knew that I met most potential clients by appointment only.

I thought I would play along. Very seriously, I told her that I could do that. I then asked her what would be the best time for her. "Nine-thirty tomorrow morning," she said without even needing to think about it.

"Fine," I said," that's wonderful. "You've got yourself a . . ." I almost said date, but then used her term ". . . an appointment."

"Thank you," she replied a little too formally. She jumped down from the chair and walked off.

The following day was Saturday. There was a part of me that cursed myself for agreeing to such an early "appointment." After all, I religiously went into the office every Saturday morning from six a.m. to noon. There was good reason for this. At those hours on the weekend, the office was empty. I had the entire place to myself without any type of interruptions. I loved the amount of leftover work I could clean up that I had left hanging from the week in that seemingly short amount of time. I also appreciated the fact that I could then make a detailed and coherent outline of what the week ahead looked like. That always got me off to a running start.

So making that play appointment with Kelley was really going to cut into my necessary work week, even though it was a Saturday. Finally, I decided that if I were really efficient, I could go into work at five a.m. instead and be done with just about everything by nine and still make it home by 9:30 for our appointment.

That night at the dinner table everyone was extremely quiet. Not only Kelley, but her brother Jared and even my wife Lisa. At the end of the evening when we were climbing into bed together, I asked Lisa about our daughter's request.

"All I know," she said as she turned off the lamp on the nightstand, "is that she wanted you to take her to the park. I volunteered to take her. But she gave me that quizzical look of hers and said, 'Mommy that would never work.' I have no idea what she means by that." Lisa rolled over and went to sleep while I stayed up a little longer and looked through several industry magazines. I found it especially difficult to sleep. I set my alarm clock appropriately so I'd be sure to make it to the office on time the following morning. Finally, I was able to sleep.

Saturday morning while I was working, I was a little irritated because I wasn't fully present as I usually was. Normally, I could throw myself into my work. Today, my mind would wander to Kelley, wondering about this "appointment." *For crying out loud,* I finally thought, *this was silly. This wasn't how I got to be successful, worrying about what's going on in my children's heads. I've got to buckle down and work, I thought.*

There was a part of me that was thankful when it was time to leave and another part that believed the following week would be a disaster because I hadn't prepared well enough for it because of this appointment with a five year old. *Your own child,* I reminded myself.

I have to give little Kelley credit. She was right on time, waiting for me at the door. I entered the house just long enough to tell my wife I was home and that we were going to the park.

Kelley was quiet on the ride there, but I was deep in thought about my strategies for the following week, so it was really only in hindsight that I could remember this. Once we got to the play area, Kelley immediately wanted to go to the swing set. She jumped on a swing and I began pushing her.

She had only swung several times when she asked me to stop pushing. Before I could ask her where she wanted to go next, she said, "I want to talk. Could you stand here in front of me, please?"

I walked around to face her and crouched down. "What's up sweetheart?" I asked, looking her in her gorgeous black eyes.

"Daddy, why don't you love me?"

I'm not sure what kind of conversation I was expecting, but it certainly wasn't one that started off with my only daughter questioning my love for her.

"Kelley, I do love you. Why would you ever think I didn't?"

"Well you never spend any time with me. And you don't spend much time with Jared or Mommy either. None of us really get to see you much. Is it something I did?"

"Of course, it's nothing you did, sweetheart. You know Daddy has to work a lot. I'm spending time with you right now," I told her.

My daughter didn't miss a beat as she said, "Daddy, you're with me, but you're not with me!"

I then told her that this morning was devoted entirely to her and whatever she wanted to do. I promised her, I would do and be fully with her. She chose a few other playground items to play on. As I sat back and watched her, my mind invariably reviewed my workload for the coming week. As I caught myself doing this, I turned my attention back to my daughter, trying to take joy in watching the innocence of play. For such a young child, I thought, she seemed to have tremendous insight. I just demonstrated to myself, that I wasn't . . . how did those spiritual gurus and New Agers put it? . . . Ah, yes! Fully in the moment!

After our appointment, we went to lunch. Again, I found my mind continually wandering to work, the upcoming appointments, sales, pitches I wanted to give people and especially the seminar I was planning. Once during this daydream, I heard a distant voice. It was Kelley.

"See Daddy, that's what I mean. You're sitting with me eating. But you're not with me. You're still at work, aren't you?"

Wow! Was I that transparent that even a five year old could tell I was at work mentally? We chatted about kindergarten. But as we talked, I realized I didn't even remember the name of her teacher. Little did I know at the moment, but this was the beginning of the universe conspiring to make me more aware of what was going on right in front of my eyes. Now, I have to tell you, I'm anything but spiritual – so it seems weird for me to even talk like this. But whatever it was, the proper alignment of the stars, a series of coincidences or just my finally being aware of my surroundings, I was only now beginning to see what my wife had been talking about for several years.

Of course, all this time, I had taken it as "nagging." She would say that I didn't spend enough time with her and the children. I would immediately get defensive and tell her that I worked my tail off every day providing for them and all of our futures.

They had everything a family could possibly want. A great car, a beautiful house, and the ability to go and buy anything they wanted at any time. They had no need to pinch pennies. It was all there. It was all laid out for them, thanks to my hard work in the insurance industry. I always ended these 'conversations' with a sarcastic, "You're welcome."

Lisa though, seldom seemed to show much gratitude. I couldn't understand it. Until now.

Chapter 2

Something Had to Change

Once Kelley had run off to her room to play, I sat down for a beer with my wife in the kitchen. I was haunted by the feeling that Lisa in some way had put Kelley up to asking this question, even though she had denied any knowledge of it just the evening before.

"How was your play date with your daughter," she began the conversation.

"You mean you don't know?" I asked, taking a sip of the cold beer.

"Now how could I possibly know? The two of you just got home and Kelley ran off to her bedroom." Lisa looked me in the eyes. I was never able to hide my feelings from her, not even from the first time we met.

"I take it there was more to it than a play date," she ventured.

I nodded. "Indeed, there was. And up until this moment, I thought you were the instigator behind it." I told her how the morning went. I even confessed that during that time my mind was, indeed, straying to my responsibilities at work, no matter how hard I tried to focus on . . . yeah . . . being in the moment with our daughter.

23

Then I told her how Kelley called me on still being at work when we were eating lunch. "I always knew she was a special girl, I just never appreciated the depth of her understanding before," I told Lisa. I was fully prepared for Lisa to tell me "I told you so." Her reaction, though, surprised – no, shocked me.

"Neither did I," Lisa said. "I'm so sorry. That's got to be a tough question to deal with." She paused a bit, took my hand and then continued. "I know that your work habits are an ongoing issue with us. But I never once in all of our . . ." She paused a moment. I knew she was searching for the right words.

"Arguments?" I offered.

"For the moment, let's call them discussions. I never once doubted that you didn't love your family. I know in my heart you work so hard because you do love us and you want to provide the best us with the best of everything. I only wanted you to think about the fact that we would rather have you home more even if it meant a little less money."

Lisa took another sip of tea. "To tell you the truth, Jerry," she continued, "Kelley would occasionally ask me the same question. She wondered if you loved her. She wondered if she had done something to make you mad at her that would cause you to spend so much time at work. It's difficult to explain your compulsive need to work to a five year old."

In any other time in our conversations, the term "compulsive" would have been enough to send me over the edge, blowing up at such a blatant exaggeration of my diligence in my career. But not today. Today, I had some soul searching to do. Perhaps I did have a compulsive habit of working. But, damn it! I was brought up on the American Work Ethic. The harder you work, so I had learned, the farther ahead you got in this country. I thought I had brought my family a long way from the lean years when we were first married. Where did I go wrong?

Lisa could see the absolute look of desperation on my face. "Honey, I'm not sure what to tell you."

I took in a deep breath and slowly let it out. "I'm not sure what to tell myself either," I answered. "But at the very least, I now know I need to spend more time with Kelley. And I can't believe I'm about to say this term, but 'quality time.'"

I got up and moved to the living room. What does any red-blooded American male do when he needs to contemplate the world? He turns the television on. Normally, when I have the TV on, I also have a magazine or a self-help book in hand. I seldom just sit and watch television.

The truth of the matter, in that moment, though, was that I wasn't just sitting and idly watching television. My mind was trying to figure out a way to dig myself out of this hole I had seemed to have gotten into with my family.

Something had to change. But what?

Chapter 3

It Played Out Like Reality TV

The following Monday at work, I went through all the motions. But it was apparent, at least to me, that I wasn't working to my full potential. Just like my mind had been at work Saturday when my body was at the playground with Kelley, my mind was now back with Kelley while my body was in the office.

I sat there regretting not feeling more in the moment with her. Wondering how many other moments I had missed. Did I really remember what her last birthday party was like? Sure I was there, but I don't even recall what we got her for a present. I can't even tell you who attended. And I certainly couldn't name any of her friends or even if they were there.

I was sitting at my desk thinking about all of this, when one of my buddies, Steve, knocked at the door to my office. I looked up, rather startled, I guess.

"Didn't mean to give you a jolt," he said, "but I couldn't help but notice you seemed preoccupied this morning. Is it that Southwest account you're trying to land. Need a sounding board?"

"Actually, it's my home life that I'm struggling with," I said, as I invited him in. I knew he wouldn't be too surprised to hear this, even though his face said differently.

"Want to talk about it?"

"Yeah, I think I do. That is if you have the time."

"I do."

"Well, let's do it over a cup of coffee somewhere other than here, then," he said. I readily agreed. Once we got to the restaurant, I explained my entire weekend to him. He listened carefully and patiently. He had the decency not to tell me, "I told you so." I can't tell you how grateful I am to people who don't stick it to me like that.

He and several other sales people had talked to me about my work habits. In the past, they had been very blunt about what they saw. They had called it my "path of destruction." At the time I dismissed them, thinking they were merely jealous about my production results.

"The truth of the matter," I said, "is that right now, I feel as if I'm not doing either my family or my job justice. For the first time in a long time, I feel . . . well . . . mediocre."

After I told him everything, I added, "And yes, I know you were one of the guys who cared enough to try to talk sense into me several years ago." Not letting him reply, I continued as if I were confessing my sins to a priest. "I even recall what you said the possible – eventual was the word you used – consequences of my continued actions would be should I not change my work habits," I said, with a slight smile. I don't know if he noticed the smile, but I felt a bit better even smiling at the situation.

"You had told me that one of three things would happen. If I kept up this pace, I would die sooner rather than later, I would burn out or my family would leave me." I sighed heavily, cupped my hands around my coffee cup and confessed, "I'm ready to listen now."

"I don't want my family to leave me," I added weakly.

Steve again told me about the coaching program that helped him get over similar hurdles in his life and career. I had heard it all before, I know. But before this weekend, I had a million reasons why I couldn't possibly do it. Well, not exactly a million, but two that I felt were good. Not enough time and I felt like I couldn't afford it.

Now, the reasons felt more like excuses. I had no alternative, no excuses. I was faced with a child who thought I didn't love her. A son who was going to need more direction than I was currently providing him and a wife . . . God knows why she stuck with me this long. If it were only the money, she could have divorced me a long time ago.

I didn't even wait until I got back to the office. Steve had given me the number of the program again and I called. It was amazingly painless. I felt relieved that I had taken a first step, even what seemed to me to be a baby step.

The result? I learned things not only about myself, but began to look deeply at the industry itself. Yes, I had my flaws, especially in thinking that I constantly needed to prove myself to my wife and children through all the hours I worked and all the money I made. As my dad used to tell me, "Hindsight is 20/20."

But in the process of my self-discovery, I learned that the insurance business set me up. It set me up to put in all those hours. It had some flaws of its own. Once I learned what the flaws were and how to overcome them, then I could begin to turn my life around.

Chapter 4

Had I Actually Worked the Best Years of My Life Away?

The coaching program turned my entire concept of my career upside down. Prior to taking the program, I worked hard – probably, looking back now -- much harder than I needed to. But at the time I had a goal – to make that exclusive one million dollar mark in sales.

I had heard that this is the mark of the true professional in the insurance business. And I was determined to achieve it. After all, I was taught that if you work hard and treat people well, you can't help but succeed.

Granted, after 20 years of 60 to 80 hour workweeks, I finally hit that coveted exclusive million dollar mark of revenue. I had dreamed of this moment for years, envisioning when I finally achieved it, I would break open a bottle of champagne to celebrate. I also believed that I'd be able to actually slow down a little, having proven myself in the business. Imagine my shock and dismay (even horror!) when I finally accomplished that milestone and discovered that a celebration – of any type – wasn't part of the game plan.

I can always make excuses for not allowing myself the champagne, but my disappointment went well beyond my ability to describe it when I realized that I couldn't slow my frenetic workaholic pace at this point. In fact, from my point of view, it appeared that I had to work even harder. After all, now I had a reputation to uphold.

What the heck, I mumbled to myself as I was surveying my options. *How did this happen?* And while I was asking questions, I couldn't help but wonder where the last twenty years had gone. I looked in the mirror the day after the announcement. Was it a coincidence I finally noticed that touch of gray in my hair?

Had I actually worked the best years of my life away?

Even now that feeling of reaching that long-sought after milestone amazes me. Instead of feeling as if the world had never witnessed a more successful person, I felt as if the achievement were an albatross around my neck. I woke up the following morning with only one possible description of what awaited me at work that day: *the daily grind.*

That day at work I met with my sales manager who rambled on about how that the million-dollar mark was only the beginning – not the capstone – of my career. He droned on about how I have to work even harder in order not to allow some young gun from stealing my thunder.

Yeah, I know I'm mixing my metaphors here, but that was really my state of mind at the time – confused, hurt and... well, I felt betrayed too.

The truth of the matter was that I didn't have any more hours to give to the business. I was tapped out, burned out, and quite frankly ready to rest on my laurels. The actual facts dictated, though, that wasn't an option.

On top of that I was grappling with the epiphany that I wasn't a good dad or husband. I felt as if my entire world were collapsing all around me. What was supposed to be a career-defining moment ended up to be a realization of all my faults.

I talked to my wife and told her what I felt. I had her read the resignation letter I had prepared. She read it and immediately tore it up. I was shocked. I thought she would be relieved. Instead, she sat me down and explained that there was a way to find the balance in my life I was searching for.

"If you quit now without discovering how to balance the different aspects of your life," she explained patiently, "you'll never resolve the situation. This same scenario will only play out in your next job, too. Confront it now, and find a solution. Your family will be here when you figure it out."

The truth of the matter was, she told me patiently, that she knew I was slowly finding that balance. I shouldn't impulsively give up my job because of my momentary feelings of inferiority. She made me promise to sit down and really look at the ways my relationship with Kelley were improving. She had me think about how I was taking a greater interest in

Jared at his young age than I had with my daughter at the same age.

Buoyed by her faith in me, I did just that. It wasn't easy though. And I'm sure during this period I stretched her patience to the breaking point. First and foremost, I set out to be that better father and husband my family deserved. Then I set a goal of realizing even greater professional and financial goals.

It didn't happen overnight. But it did happen. It took four years of soul searching and asking tough questions – of myself and the insurance industry itself. I questioned everything I had learned, everything I had believed.

The result was that in those four years I not only learned how to actually be a dad to my children and a husband to Lisa, I actually quadrupled my revenue results. And believe it or not, I did it in half the time I had been spending.

Cracking the Code: The Five Fatal Flaws of the Business

I was able to do this because I was finally able to crack that code of insurance sales. I discovered what I called its Five Fatal Flaws of the insurance industry. I learned the "games" the business played with its agents and brokers. And I learned the built in problems that if you don't compensate for them not only will be fatal for your career, but they could prove crippling – if not fatal – to the industry itself.

Once I figured this out, it took no time at all to turn the tables on them. Now, don't misunderstand me, these were not lessons that I learned all at once. No great epiphany hit me; nothing came down from the heavens and bestowed this all-knowing power down on me at once. It took me years to eventually figure this out. The important point is, though, that I eventually did figure them out. And I like to explain this merely by stating two words: The C.R.A.P

Chapter 5

What The C.R.A.P is Happening in the Insurance

Sales Business?

What The C.R.A.P.?

The question represents more than merely an interjection of my amazement once I analyzed the industry. It's what I see actually happening in the business. The phrase is an acronym for what I consider to be the Five Fatal Flaws of the insurance industry. Once I was able to recognize these flaws and overcome these flaws, my continued success became effortless.

The acronym stands for:

The – Trust
C   -- Commodity
R   -- Roving targets
A   -- Agency death spiral
P   -- Professionalism

Trust: Difficult to Find In the Business

The "T" in The C.R.A.P. system is probably the biggest problem the industry has going today. And it's the first aspect of the insurance business I began to dig into – once I felt compelled to change my life. I couldn't help but notice the reactions of others when I told them I was an insurance agent.

The final straw for me was the time my wife and I were at a small cocktail party given by one of her friends. I was introduced to a businessman who immediately asked what I did for a living. When I told him I sold insurance, he couldn't hide his disdain or his nervousness.

He quickly looked around the room and said, "You know, I'm really not in the market for any right now. Excuse me, I think I see someone I haven't talk to in years. It's been nice talking to you." He couldn't get away from me fast enough.

The sad part of that story is that I had no intention of using that party as leverage to gain customers. Later that evening I cornered the gentleman. Boy, I swear I saw beads of sweat rolling down his face.

"I believe you misconstrued my presence at the party tonight," I said, trying to sound casual. "I had no intention of turning my wife's friends wonderful cocktail party into a platform for my networking. I am here at the request of my wife in the capacity of her husband and friends of the host and hostess. Nothing more."

You should have seen the look on his face. He turned ten shades of red. "I'm . . . well . . . I never . . ."

I stopped him before he could finish. "That's okay," I said. "There's no need to apologize. It probably doesn't surprise you that I get that reaction all the time. My wife and I are leaving right now, but I really hope we have another chance just to talk." With that, I shook his hand and walked over to my wife.

Lisa gave me a puzzled look. "I just wanted to set the record straight with him. I know it doesn't matter, but I really am not a vulture. I wanted him to know I had no intention of talking insurance tonight. Good grief! It was such a wonderful respite not to talk about my job this evening."

Lisa smiled at me and said, "I never saw a man run from a situation as fast as he did."

"Welcome to my world."

A Necessary Evil

The insurance industry is nothing more than a necessary evil to many individuals. Everyone knows they need to purchase insurance, yet few persons really feel satisfied with their choice. Making regular payments on insurance seems to rank up there in appreciation with paying utility bills.

Wait! At least with utility bills, you know you're getting a service every month. You can at least see the results of our payments. How many can say that about their insurance payments?

Beginning to see a reason for the skepticism? People naturally ask the question, "What are those companies doing with all that money?" Hmm. No wonder there's an underlying, unsettling tension of distrust in this business.

Stephen Covey, author of the seminal, "The 7 Habits of Highly Effective People," explained trust is "the glue of life. It's the most essential ingredient in effective communication. It's the fundamental principle that holds all relationships."

That really should come as no revelation, but all the same it's something every insurance agent should keep uppermost in his or her mind. If you've spent years earning the trust of your clients, you may be disappointed to learn that the insurance industry does little to nothing to help you.

In fact, if you were the least bit paranoid, you might believe, at first glance, the sales business takes pride in its reputation for not garnering trust from its customers. It is, after all, a field that is looked at skeptically by far too many.

People buy insurance because it's necessary. They choose their provider, all too often, based on the concept of the "least of the evils" available to them.

Don't believe me? You should have been in the auditorium when I spoke to a group of entrepreneurs from both the U.S. and Canada about the subject. I purposely talked about the subject of trust.

"Do you trust the insurance industry?"

That was the first question I asked them. Nothing like clearing the air right at the start, I figured. Besides, I wanted to bring home a vital point. Not surprisingly, when I asked for a show of hands of those who did trust the industry, not a single hand went up. A few people in the front several rows glanced behind them and smirked.

"It Frosts Me My Claim Was Denied."

Not willing to leave the topic there, I continued on. "Why the distrust?" I asked. At first no one was offering much in the way of answers, but eventually one entrepreneur answered. "Frankly, I really don't have a clue how the insurance business works. What I do know, though, is that every month I pay my premium. I do this faithfully so that should I need to file a claim I can be covered.

So it really frosts me that on the rare occasions I actually file a claim. Some yahoo somewhere denies it. Tell me, exactly what am I paying for? How can any company expect to build a trust with its customers when it pulls a stunt like that?"

After he spoke, several others were willing to open up and talk about their insurance "experiences." One gentleman said that he trusted the process of buying insurance only when he could "pit" insurance agents against one another.

I asked what he meant by that. I personally envisioned him throwing several agents into a Romanesque coliseum armed with nothing but swords and shields. "Let the fighting begin!" he would yell. And the agent who came out alive won his business.

He explained that he would shop every year and relay to one agent the lowest quote he had already received from another. If he could come in lower great. He then promised to get back to him. In the meantime, he went hunting to see if anyone could bring in a quote even lower than that for similar coverage.

"What if I told you," I asked after hearing his method, "that the business is set up so that it's not in the best interest of your agent to give you the lowest price?" Groans resonated throughout the auditorium. A few individuals responded with a disgusted "I knew it. I always suspected it."

"Here's why," I explained to them that the more they paid for their insurance the larger the agent's commission check would be. In the same vein, the less they paid, that would be reflected by a smaller commission check.

Finally concluding the explanation, I asked them, "How does that make you feel? Do you feel these incentives are aligned? By that I mean do you think your agent is getting compensated to look after your interests and your particular situation?" The auditorium erupted in conversation.

One entrepreneur sprung out of his chair, stood and loudly declared, "That's it! I knew there was a reason why I didn't trust this business. I just couldn't put my finger on it. That's exactly the reason I'm forced to shop for a new insurance program every two to three years."

"Explain yourself further," I said. "I'd like to hear what you do."

"Well, it's simple," he said, as all the other individuals in the audience turned to look at him. "When I get a new agent, he's always real responsive. You know, ready to go that extra mile to help me reduce my costs. When that happens I feel as if I've found that pot of gold at the end of the rainbow.

"But then the year or two following that," he explains, "he just can't bring my premiums down any more. He's done everything within his power, he tells me." He paused for a moment before continuing as if he were trying to compose his anger. "Now, I understand why. If he reduced my premiums any more, he'd be cutting into his own commission. And I'm already a fish on a hook. He doesn't need to hook me in. Basically his work for me is done. He was concerned about my bottom line as long as it was helping his bottom line."

"Bingo!" I replied, "You're exactly right. And that is what the bedrock is when it comes to that lack of trust we were talking about. The way in which the foundation of the insurance business itself is set up is fundamentally flawed. Basically the incentives are misaligned and backwards."

Groans of recognition and realization reverberated throughout the room. "The only way this picture ends," I told them, "is in a win-lose proposition. Somebody has to lose. Either the customer or the sales agent. At this point, you both can't win."

In a nutshell, the way the industry has been historically run, either you, the purchaser of the insurance wins, by paying lower premiums and reducing your agent's commissions or your agent wins and you lose. This occurs when your agent receives a handsome commission based on you paying larger premiums."

"That's so wrong on so many levels," I continued, "this business should never be set up like a children's teeter totter. I'm on top now because you're paying more. I'm near the ground now because you're saving money. It may be a fun playground ride, but it's a lousy way to conduct business."

"Instead, it should always work out so that the better it is for you, the customer, the better it is for your insurance agent. No questions asked. Case closed. Only when your incentives as a customer are aligned with mine as an agent can everyone win."

Creating a Win-Win Situation

Everyone in the room certainly agreed. Then I asked them, "If I could show you a way to change the incentive model to align both the agent's and the customer's incentives so that everyone benefited from your purchase, would you be interested?"

Of course, they all said yes. They were all entrepreneurs. They weren't naïve about the needs of their agents to make money. Heck, that's what they were all about -- making money themselves. In the next breath, though, they expressed skepticism that it could be done.

"That's how I work with my clients," With that, I transformed an indifferent and, in fact, a potentially hostile group of people into a gathering of conceivably, grateful customers. With that simple opening exercise, they were much more receptive to listening to what I had to say.

Of course, there's always one contrary individual in the room – perhaps this is the insurance agent's equivalent to the stand up comedian's heckler. In any case, he said, even before he heard the details, that his mind was closed.

He said he would continue to pit the agent's up against each other in an insurance gladiator's contest. Of course, this is also the same person who said when he did file a claim it was denied.

"Perhaps your method," I said, trying to be as kind as possible, "isn't really working for you." Many in attendance laughed. "You may want to re-think your strategy."

At first the gentleman appeared genuinely upset and defensive, then he let his guard down. His body slumped a bit and admitted, "Maybe I do need to rethink it." And he sat down.

It was also at this point, that some individuals opened up about their goals and plans in purchasing insurance – and why they seemed at odds with the goals, needs and nudging of his agent.

"To be truthful," one person said, "I've been nothing but frustrated lately with my agent. Quite frankly, there are some things I really didn't intend to purchase insurance for. I wanted to self-insure these items. Now, that I have a better idea of this structure thing, I can see why he seems as if he's fighting me tooth and nail."

"The bottom line is apparently, he doesn't get paid for just giving me advice. He only gets paid if he sells me something. So why the heck should he help me self-insure some things? I'm literally taking money out of his pocket, aren't I?"

By now, the room was buzzing with any number of private conversations. People were turning to each other no doubt recounting their own experiences with various insurance agents throughout the years. At some point, I knew I would have to bring order to the meeting, but right now, I felt the energy in the room, it was great. I was pleased with their new understanding of the situation.

You see, I feel confident that this group of entrepreneurs got it. They know that as part of doing business, we insurance agents needed compensation for our services. I also knew that they had no problems with this arrangement. They expected us to get paid for our services. But at the same time, they needed more. Namely, our advice and support equally as much. And they seemed to think we were already getting compensated for that as well.

Changes on the Horizon

The current way the commission structure is set up is nothing but archaic, to say the least. All this does is continue the misalignment of incentives, which, in turn, only leads to a win-lose situation and eventually a breach of trust between agent and customer.

There is hope that soon – very soon – this structure, which is out of step with the twenty-first century will fade into oblivion. The insurance industry will have to change. I can already see this occurring. Slowly, but it's happening. There is an ever-increasing amount of transparency when it comes to commissions.

In some areas, I already see the shift occurring. Take the area of employee benefits, for example. Anyone now can access an employer's 5500 form. This document outlines the agent's or broker's commission.

My own home insurance, for example, is with Chubb. When my renewal came in the mail, there was also a notice that I could visit their web site to see what the commission my agent was making.

And in the United Kingdom, believe it or not, insurance policies are now sold without the addition of the agent's commission. In other words, the consumer is shown what the net cost of the insurance is prior to the addition of the commission. The agent is then in a position in which he or she must add in his commission.

The insurance industry, as a whole, has never been really comfortable revealing this to customers. And from what I can gather most agents and brokers feel very uncomfortable doing business this way.

Why? I'm not sure. But I sense that there's a pervading fear floating around that if customers were aware of the amount of the commission their agent was making, they would try to negotiate the agent to a smaller commission.

That's a shame. Call me idealistic if you'd like, but I firmly believe that our industry should be at the top of the charts when it involves affecting our clients' bottom line.

It's also a shame that we're not seen in the same light as the legal and accounting industries. Those working in these areas are seen as true professionals. For some reason, insurance agents seem to be on a rung or more below them. Personally, I keep coming back to the trust issue. The "T" in what The C.R.A.P system.

Now some of you may argue that we are. Let's be realistic about this, however. How often does any customer or client pit attorney's costs against another or accountants' prices against each other?

It just doesn't make a whole lot of sense to me that it occurs as much as it does in the insurance industry.

Creating a Win-Win Situation

It's not an easy fix. I have to really work at creating a win-win situation when it comes to my customer's needs and my needs. But I will tell you it really is worth the effort. I make a conscious decision to create this atmosphere. As you see from my seminar with the best and brightest entrepreneurs, it took more than a little work.

Creating an atmosphere in which a win-win situation can blossom also means I'm sticking my neck out. I'm taking risks most agents aren't taking. I choose to make a conversation that will set us down the road to a specific destination. While I may be skipping down the path of the Yellow Brick Road, I could just as easily be walking into that coliseum that so many other agents are subjected to.

More often than not, when I work closely with a client in this manner, we can come up with a financial arrangement that works quite well for both of us. What occurs during these conversations is a natural alignment of interests. We both find incentives to create the best deal possible. This shows not only in my bottom line, but in my customer's as well.

As the issue of clarity becomes more widespread, each agency will need to approach the situation in its own way.

Each agency will eventually have to sort out exactly what this new way of conducting business means to their employees and their customers.

Easy Does It!

Let's get one thing straight before we go too much farther. This is not an easy issue for many individuals to talk about. It's an issue, however, that desperately needs to be addressed. Never think for a moment that a flat, across-the-board answer works for all. It doesn't.

One reason for this involves the wide variety of rules and regulations depending on the state in which you're working which regulate insurance compensation. Personally, it took me a full two years to plow through all the red tape, as it were, in order to clarify everything with the department of insurance superintendent. I had to be absolutely sure I was in compliance with the law.

Action Steps

This approach can work for you. Where do you start, though? The following action steps can get you started regardless of where you live:

1. Do your clients trust you?

If you're not sure, think about how many of them "shop around" searching for better rates. The fewer of them that do this, the higher their trust level in you. Have you ever really asked their opinion about what they like – and more importantly, what they dislike – about the risk management and risk financing process?

2. What structures can you create and then implement in your agency that would allow you to do what is right for your client without you and your agency losing valuable revenue?

While saving your clients money is important, it's worth little if it hurts your or your firm's bottom line.

3. How soon will compensation transparency be mandated through the actions of your competition or by government competition?

4. Do your clients and prospects have a clear understanding of how the industry actually functions?

Chapter 6

The Danger of Commodity Thinking

As my coaching program took its hold on me, I was beginning, however slowly, to truly reunite with my family – especially my daughter.

Soon a year had passed and we were celebrating her birthday. I recall this distinctly. While it was her sixth birthday, it was the first party of Kelley's that I had attended from start to finish.

It was the first time I had worn those silly little party hats. You know the ones that make you look like you should be sitting in a corner because you misbehaved at school?

My attendance didn't go unnoticed by my family either – especially Kelley.

"Dad," she said, after all the family and friends left, "I can't believe you stayed for the whole thing. Thank you." She threw her little arms around as much of me as she could reach.

I looked into her big black eyes and felt that I had won her love back. I was definitely on the right track.

Later that night, my wife and I were lying in bed. "Good job, Jerry," she told me. "I'm not sure how hard that party was for you to sit through, but you did appear to enjoy yourself."

I turned to her and gently kissed her on the cheek. "I did enjoy it," I replied. "And I enjoyed receiving a great big thank you from my daughter."

Shortly after that birthday party, I was destined to learn the second fatal flaw of the insurance industry. The "C" in The C.R.A.P. system.

"C" Stands for Commodity

And trust me on this one, that's the very last thing you want your prospects and clients to think of when your name and services come to mind. If you suspect it is right now . . . well, that's understandable. The industry sets us up for this.

Whether you truly believe it or not, the fact exists: Every agent has to some extent coached and taught our clients and prospects to commoditize us. A commodity is, as you're well aware, a product. It's the policies we sell. But, in fact, we offer so much more to our customers. We offer them expertise, counseling and advice based on our years in the business. And we really are the experts when it comes to this business. So why do we sell ourselves short?

I did exactly this for at least 20 years. The result? Well, aside from the fact that they really did view me as a commodity, the adverse side effects on my part could be summed up in one word: frustration.

I saw with my own eyes that regardless of our actions, or the array of services we provided, my agency would inevitably get outbid on policies and lose that particular client. The client I had spent so long in cultivating, attracting and thought was sure of retaining. He was gone in a heartbeat.

When You Live by the Price, You'll Inevitably Die by the Price

One thing is for sure. You'll never stand alone if you play the commodity game. There's much competition in this area.

Regardless of your intent or how much you *believe* you value your clients, none of that is relevant as long as you're being drawn into a pricing war to see which agent can supply your client or prospect with the least expensive policies.

By the way, you'll eventually end up losing, though, because there's always someone out there "gunning for you." There's always some agent who'll be able to beat your price. When you live by the price, you'll inevitably die by the price.

While there's also some agent or broker out there waiting to pounce on you, to beat your price, remember that not every agent is going to do this in an ethical manner.

Oh, your client will figure this out sooner or later. Unfortunately, it usually takes them a good year with the other agent until they finally realize it.

And what are you doing during that year? Scrambling to fill the void of that lost revenue!

Total Cost of Risk – TCOR -- and My Wake-Up Call

I had spent fifteen years in the insurance business before I had ever heard that term: *Total Cost of Risk.* Many just refer to it by its initials TCOR. At least, this encounter was the first time I stopped to consider what it truly meant.

In basic terms, it's the concept of how to quantify the amount of risk a client had. Knowing this allowed me to change the way I talked with clients. I was able to go beyond just calculating the cost of their policies. This knowledge allowed me to actually help them keep score, if you will, and determine their true costs.

I finally saw the light when we hired a retired risk manager to complete a gap analysis of our own business and personal risks. Imagine our shock when we discovered that we had $28 million in gaps. Twenty-eight million dollars!

No, these gaps were neither inflated nor imagined. They were real existing gaps that were the result of the various types of risks we had exposed ourselves to – both professionally and personally.

Ironically, we – industry professionals – were guilty of performing the exact same practice that we complained our customers did to us: buying insurance protection as if it were a commodity. We bought based on the best price without a true understanding of the various types of risk we were exposed to. If we had carried that philosophy much farther, it could have bankrupted us.

Instead, we faced up to the problem, discussed the best methods of mitigating much of the risk, eliminating what we needed to and retooling the rest. Soon, we had an affordable plan. And when it was all said and done we accomplished it for less than a $25,000 increase in our total expenses.

Talk about knowing how my clients felt. At that moment, I did. I realized how close we were to "commoditizing" ourselves right out of business. I've found, though, that everything happens for a reason. From the playground appointment with my daughter Kelley to the huge gaps in our own risks. All events seem to work to teach me lessons in my life.

While it may have been a difficult lesson to learn, it was not one I was going to soon forget. And that was I finally learned the best way to approach a client's risk and have a productive discussion. I was able to talk intelligently about his overall risk as well as the best methods to reduce, eliminate or finance it. I became much more comfortable about talking about how we as agents were paid for the least valuable of all of our activities – buying and selling insurance policies.

In the same vein, I didn't hesitate to tell them that I wasn't getting paid at all for the most valuable of our services: our knowledge, experience and wisdom in helping to protect them.

In reality, calling this a "wake-up" call is quite an understatement. The $28 million gap in our agency's own risk caused a transformation of seismic portions in my thinking and my approach to my career.

Action Steps:

1. Are you coaching your clients and prospects to commoditize you?

2. What steps are you taking to make yourself stand apart from your competitors?

3. What percentage of your time are you competing solely on the price of your policies?

4. Can you intelligently talk to your clients and prospects about why using only the price of the policies of the insurance policies can adversely affect their bottom line?

5. Realistically speaking, what is your success rate with regard to winning new accounts and retaining your existing ones?

Chapter 7

It's Hard to Hit a Roving Target

"You can't sell what John Smith buys until you can see through his eyes."

As I learned to balance my work and my home life, I had what I jokingly call my "mystical" experience, an epiphany of sorts. I became much better at seeing my actions through the eyes of my family. In effect, you might say I was empathizing with them.

First, I have to predicate this experience on the realization that they – Lisa, Kelley and little Jared – loved me. And they loved me for me – not because I brought home a good paycheck, or because I was able to supply them with the latest in technological gadgets or any other material reasons. For me, that in itself was a mystical experience.

Once I realized that, I was able to imagine "what if I was a five-year-old child who didn't get to see enough of his dad?" I was able to ask questions that were more in tuned with her thinking.

I don't mention this just as an aside. It seems that events occur in our lives for reasons – and seldom do you see an isolate event just dangling in the universe. As I learned how to look at life through my daughter's eyes, I began to do more of this.

Similarly, I began to see my customers' businesses through their eyes more clearly. It didn't happen all at once and it really didn't come particularly easy to me, I must say. But the important thing was that I eventually "got it."

That's more than what the majority of the producers can say. They really have no method to see through their clients' eyes. It's a sad commentary that the insurance industry is fraught with a host of assumptions that we know what our clients and prospects need and even what they want based solely on our skills and knowledge.

You noticed, I even mentioned this in the last chapter. Now don't get me wrong. To a large extent that's very accurate. We have knowledge and expertise that they don't. But there's another piece to that puzzle we often overlook. And that's the very real expertise and knowledge they have in their particular business and their circumstances. Quite frankly, we don't know a thing about that.

I've always prided myself on staying abreast of all the developments in our industry. Anytime a new tool or a solution appeared, I (along with many others in the insurance business) learned as much as I could as quickly as possible. I was well prepared to offer it to my clients.

Or so I thought I was well prepared.

In reality, I found that having the knowledge of my industry alone was having only half of the knowledge I needed. There was still a gap in my education. Initially, I was too blind to see it, I was so busy sopping up the new products (dare I say commodities?) so that I could "puke out" solutions for my clients. Ironically, I was excited about providing them solutions without even knowing their problems.

By the way, this is just one more reason why the industry is backwards. By doing this, I invited my clients to view me as a commodity, now didn't I?

My Transformation in the Insurance Industry

Before I continue any farther, though, let me tell you about how I evolved as an agent and how these experiences affected me. Then you'll have a better understanding of my "mystical" experience.

During my initial years in the business, I mostly sold life insurance. I received a good deal of training, especially when it involved prospecting and understanding the ratio of contacts to actual sales. There was an aspect of the life insurance business I didn't care for, though. This was learning the actual sales pitch, calling on the people and then selling them a product without ever learning their needs.

In particular, I felt that I never really learned how to ask the right questions to get to the heart of their needs. This was an art I never mastered. There's probably a good reason for this. I was so focused on learning about my product. Since no one really insisted I learn this, I assumed that perhaps it wasn't as important as I thought it was.

On top of that I became obsessed with "playing the numbers game" – discovering who actually needed the product I was selling at just the right time in their lives. I didn't find this game very entertaining, because, quite frankly, other than the products I was selling, I didn't have any solutions for them.

A More Fun Approach Opened Up to Me

However, the following fifteen years or so turned out to be – dare I say? – More fun. And because I looked on it in a different light, I experienced more success with it (of course putting sixty to eighty hours a week into it didn't hurt). I moved into working for my family agency. We had four departments: personal lines, commercial lines, employee benefits and bonds.

I could feel my opportunities growing. After all, I had more products to sell. Just about everyone needs to buy some type of insurance coverage. This meant that my list of prospects just expanded exponentially – at least in my mind.

What I didn't bank on in the midst of my initial elation was the competition. Regardless of what I knew about insurance coverage some competitor always seemed to know more. That, I was beginning to learn, was how it was always going to be. (But it took me a while to realize that. Yet, another epiphany!)

Let me tell you, this lesson was without a doubt one of the toughest ones of my entire career to learn. It was, also, one that I desperately needed to learn.

I was meeting with one of my toughest clients. I called on him on this particular visit to sell him one of our new umbrella policies. I had my sales spiel prepared. I knew exactly why he needed it. Or so I thought.

Hold on right there, young man," he said before I could get very far into my presentation. Funny, when I practiced it, I hadn't practiced interruptions into it. His comment took me aback. "Why in blue blazes do you believe for one moment I need this policy?

"Quite frankly, I really don't care if this policy makes sense to you," he continued. "If it's not aligned with my needs and wants it's worthless to me." He paused a beat and I opened my mouth to talk, but never gave me the chance. He continued on.

"I'm positive you have no idea what my needs or my wants are. You've never asked me what they are!"

I found I couldn't argue with this. I hadn't asked him what he needed. I scrambled to defend myself, but it was useless. He finally stopped me again emphasizing his point even further, "You're not listening to me. Let me make myself perfectly clear on this matter. I'm not about to buy this product until and unless you and I can discuss intelligently what I need and what I want."

Again he paused. As if I was supposed to say something. I was speechless. So he prompted me. "Okay, fire away! What questions do you want to ask me?"

My client had effectively called my bluff. I spent all my time learning my end of the business. I learned all the bells and whistles of this policy, without knowing if he even needed them.

In addition to calling my bluff, he chiseled down to having me doubt my own integrity. "If you were a medical doctor," he admonished me, "I could actually accuse you of malpractice." I'm sure I couldn't hide the look on my face as I asked why that was.

"Because, a doctor can't write a prescription without first making a diagnosis. What you just did was try to write me a prescription for some ailment in my business that you don't even know really exists or not."

It's actually one of the first lessons that many direct marketers and other sales personnel learn. But I failed to learn it. It's understanding the difference between "features" and "benefits." I knew all the features of the policy, but I knew nothing about him, so I couldn't turn the features into how they were "benefits" for him.

As you may recall, I told you my formative years in the business were spent in life insurance where I really never developed a strategy of learning my customers' needs. It came back to bite me here.

You can guess how that sales pitch ended. He tossed me out on my rear. He did give me a slight reprieve. He told me not to come back until I could figure out a way to learn more about his needs and wants. He didn't slam the door in my face forever.

I had commoditized myself.

The Quest

Talk about an epiphany. At that moment, I fully came to realize that I was not seeing through the eyes of my customers. Not by a long shot. That's the moment I vowed never to suffer such humiliation again – not that I didn't have it coming mind you.

Like a modern-day Don Quixote I set out on a quest to discover the best way to learn my clients' needs. I set my sights on learning what I failed to learn when I was selling life insurance: asking good questions of my clients' needs. Unless I could discover how to do this, I would always remain in the commodities game. That field was too crowded with competitors to suit me.

Playing the Game of D.A.R.T.S.

I thought long and hard about this gap in my education. And I decided that this is just another fatal flaw. The way the business is structured, it makes discovering your clients' and prospects' needs difficult. If you've ever went out hunting you know how difficult it is to shoot a roving target. Our industry typically views our customers' needs as roving targets.

In fact, I created my own analogy that likens the process to a game of darts, albeit a most unusual and difficult game of darts. Here's how this unique game is structured.

First, the customer blindfolds you. Then, like in the game Pin the Tail on the Donkey, your prospect spins you around. Now you're dizzy and disoriented and your prospect is standing across the room from you holding a dartboard. You, by the way, are in possession of five darts. Just five darts.

If you can hit the dartboard considering all the conditions just created, you receive the opportunity to conduct business with him. And, oh yes, did I mention that while you're in the process of throwing the first dart, he can move anywhere around the room? Yeah, he can.

If, however, you throw a dart and you miss, well, the prospect receives the opportunity to move further away from you – in effect, to distance himself from you. Each time you miss, in fact, he gets to move farther from you. You throw until you have no darts left.

Realistically, what do you think your chances are of actually doing business with this prospect? Small to none would be my guess. At least those would be my chances. Does it surprise you to know that's how most of us are working? We're trying to throw darts at *Roving* objects. That's why this fatal flaw is the "R" in The C.R.A.P. system. Not only is it not fair; it's not a very efficient use of anyone's time or energy.

Let's Change the Rules Slightly

What if we changed the rules of the dart game even just a little? What if we play without wearing the blindfold? Now we can see where the prospect stands. He's still in control of the dartboard. But instead of the five darts determining whether you can do business with him, they now questions you may ask him about his needs and wants.

Each time you ask a good, intelligent question about his needs and wants and you receive an answer, he moves closer to you. After you've asked five good questions and received five good answers, then the two of you are standing face to face.

And this positioning signals a "bonus round" (of course, every good game show has a bonus round!). This consists of you passing off the darts to your prospect and asking him to place them on the bull's eye on the board.

The game ends with you knowing what your prospect needs and wants. Your job now becomes supplying him with a solution, or at the very least, connecting your client with some type of solution, whether it's you or another provider of some type.

Oddly enough, I've named this process D.A.R.T. It stands for:

D – Discovery
A – Analyze
R – Re-design, tool and affirm
T – Track

The way it works is straightforward. In the discovery phase, you ask questions that are designed to determine whether you and your client or prospect is in alignment. The answers will show you the best way in which you can help him.

The analyze phase consists of you analyzing the information provided by the client or prospect with an eye toward matching up his needs and wants with the current potential solutions you have.

In the re-design, tool and affirm phase, you present your client with a new plan that will best aid him to go forward.

Without a doubt the most critical phase, the track portion, enables you to show the client the results of your working together. It's here that you can quantify the impact your solutions made on his bottom line.

With this set of rules, you're much closer than ever to creating a win-win situation for you and your prospects. On top of that, you're much less likely to find some gunslinger coming into town set on undercutting your price. And even if one shows up, your customer is less likely to respond positively to his overtures.

Action Steps:

1. Do you currently have a consistent method to discover what your clients' wants and needs are?

Or are you like I was, playing an insane and largely unwinnable game of darts – blindfolded?

2. Are you guilty of writing out prescriptions for your clients' business ailments without making a proper diagnosis?

3. How do you currently determine your clients' and prospects' priorities?

Do you even know what they are?

4. How do you keep score with your clients? In other words, how do you track your impact on their business?

Do they know if you're favorably affecting their bottom line?

Chapter 8

What The C.R.A.P.? The Agency Death Spiral:

What You Can Do to Stop It!

"Misaligned incentives always eventually create a win-lose proposition."

Jerry Lujan

You undoubtedly learned, just as I did when I entered the sales industry, that agents and brokers distributed our "value added services," essentially for free. When we did this, so our mentors and teachers told us, we would naturally sell more insurance policies (the commodities) and make more money.

In theory, this sounds wonderful, especially if you're just starting out in the business and are . . . well, naïve to how the industry really works. This advice makes sense. At least it did for the first few years I was in the business.

I'm willing to challenge that advice – and in a big way. Not only do I believe it's a misguided strategy for individual agents to use, I am adamant that it's also a strategy that's killing the insurance industry as a whole.

You recall earlier in our discussion, how we spoke of one of the fatal flaws of the industry as being a lack of trust between agent and client. This is illustrated in the client's apparent need to shop their insurance agent and carrier frequently. While no one in the business has actually told them, their intuition tells them that we are paid a commission.

Sometimes I believe that insurance companies are doing their darnedest to keep its agents and brokers perpetually tethered to this insane and archaic way of doing business. Why? Just look in the past several years, the number of value-added services that the industry has added. Services that we, as agents, are actually giving away.

The more value added services we offer, the greater the costs of doing business becomes. It's a double-whammy from my perspective at least. Here's the kicker: When an agency gets really good at implementing these "free" services, the result is usually they lower the client's risk. And you know what happens next! The client's premium is lower, which in turn actually decreases the overall revenues of the agency. Wow! Talk about a vicious circle. It really is causing an Agency Death Spiral – the "A" in The C.R.A.P. system.

Let's take a closer look at how this works. Let's assume a client is currently paying $500,000 in insurance premiums. Let's also assume – for the sake of simplicity – the average commission on these premiums is 12 percent. That makes the annual commission $60,000.

Next, let's assume you've invested in the value added service. You "gave them away" to the client in exchange for his business. It really doesn't matter what these services specifically are. But they would probably look something like loss control actuary, experience modifier, claims, and the like.

It's not a stretch to say that these services represent thousands of investment dollars. It's not even a stretch to imagine that – being the incredibly talented salesperson you are – these services decreased your client's premiums by 20 percent.

Yep! You did a good job. And in a moment, you'll see how the industry you represent is about to reward all your hard work. A decrease of 20 percent means your client's new premium is $400,000. Your new commission – based on the average 12 percent we spoke of earlier – is now $48,000.

Congratulations! You've Worked Yourself into a Pay Cut!

It's true! By doing everything the industry required of you, you've made your client immensely happy, but, in the process, brought your own commission tumbling down by 20 percent. What's wrong with this picture?

How does it feel to be in mid-flight of an agency death spiral? Now you're getting a bird's eye view of what a win-lose scenario this can create. And you, my friend, are on the losing end.

But wait! It Gets Worse!

I can hear you groan all the way over here. Right now, you probably can't imagine how. I'm here to bring you the bad news.

Let's fast forward to Year Three with this client. Just as the industry expects and you've been trained to do, you're continuing to give − literally − more value added services to this particular client. After all, he's beginning to get nervous. You think he's on the verge of shopping around for better pricing.

This time, you're able to reduce his costs by $100,000, making his new premium even more affordable: $300,000.

You're probably already ahead of me and are calculating what your commission would be at 12 percent. Well, scratch that number. Because in these three years, the insurance carriers are getting even more competitive and they've reduced your commission down to 10 percent for this newly signed premium contract.

You read that right! Now, your client pays $300,000 a year in premiums and of that you receive 10 percent for all of your hard work. Your new commission is now $30,000. So, from the start of the first year to the start of the third year, thanks to the structure of the industry, you've worked harder and . . . reduced your commission by 50 percent.

Instead of the $60,000 you first received when you signed this client, you're now only receiving $30,000 and giving away even more added value services.

Here's My Ethical Dilemma Thrown in for Good Measure!

If you believe I'm inflating numbers or exaggerating the gravity of the situation, you're wrong. I'm doing neither. In fact, I've yet to add in the third factor in all of this. The factor that not only is financially troubling, but was ethically problematic for me.

The illustration I've just shown you was drawn from my experience. All of that occurred. My commission after two years really did decrease by 50 percent. I just rounded the numbers for the ease of explanation.

The largest troubling factor in this, though, involved the ethics of my handling the situation. Here's how this portion played out.

The existing carrier for these policies was paying the 10 percent commission rate. But I found a competitor who came in with a significantly lower premium for my client. The kicker: it only paid a 2 percent commission.

Had I sold this policy to my customer, the lower commission would have reduced the agency's revenue by yet another $12,000. That would have sent our overall revenue tumbling even further – down to $18,000. Considering this alternative, let's look at these numbers from this perspective. In those two short years the agency had the potential to go from a revenue of $60,000 down to a total revenue of $18,000 on those very same policies. That's a whopping decrease of $42,000 or about 70 percent!

The client, however, didn't go with the lowest-priced insurance carrier. We fully explained the differences in the claims philosophy and other aspects of the carrier's services, which convinced him to retain his existing insurance.

The sad part of this story is that it really did occur to me *not to show* my client the reduced rates of the one carrier solely based on the amount of revenue the agency would have lost if he had bought it. That's definitely not the recommended way to create trust. But all I could see was the slow death spiral of the agency.

You Ain't Seen Nothin' Yet!

Stop! Because I haven't quite finished this story. Just when you think the pieces of this puzzle couldn't get possibly more scrambled and more bizarre, they do. Here's how: It's called the producer's sales model and is intended to create competition solely on commission or fee reduction.

Unfortunately, there are many producers who – in my opinion are desperate enough to shut their brains down for a while – to "compete" by visiting prospects, figuring out approximately what the commission is that the prospect is paying and then promising to do everything you're currently doing for your client and more for much less.

How do I know? I've lost several accounts this way. I'm about to tell you about a rather large account that fell through my fingers in this fashion.

The client was a contractor who was paying $750,000 in total premiums. That was down from the $1,000,000 he was originally paying during the first year we worked with him. In the previous three years, we had reduced his premiums by a $250,000 – a quarter of a million dollars!

And yes, you guessed it. We did this through offering many value added services for free. We incorporated a behavioral safety program into the services and even assigned a claims advocate from our office.

In those three years, his workers compensation experience mod went from 1.25 to 0.85. Not only that, but his losses plummeted from $800,000 to less than $250,000. That didn't appear to be the final number in loss reduction either.

When we first signed this customer our compensation for this was approximately $120,000. The final year our commission was down to $90,000 for all these savings. Right there you can see how adding these services doesn't necessarily translate into a larger commission for the agency. No win-win alignment here.

Despite this reduction in our commission, I was thrilled with what we did for him. Naturally, I thought he, too, was thrilled. I also thought he knew how hard we worked together to make all of this happen.

The Phone Call that Transformed my Outlook

When I received the phone call from him, it struck me like a lightning bolt in a thunderstorm. To say his news caught me off guard was an understatement.

That phone conversation is indelibly planted in my mind. "Jerry, you and your agency have done a great job for us over the past three years," he said, puffing me up a bit. "I know you've done everything you said that you could have possibly done – and then some."

"So, it's not really easy to tell you that I've changed my coverage to go with another agent." At this point, I thought my client was joking.

Then he specifically added, "I'm not kidding, Jerry. As much as it hurts me, I have to do this for the sake of my business in general."

I remember asking why. It just didn't make any sense to me.

"I found an agent who can save me $65,000 over and above what you've saved me." He then paused and added slowly, "I don't know how to say this any other way, but I feel as if you've been overcharging me these past three years."

Wow! Talk about a kick in the pants!

By now in this telephone conversation I'm ticked off. I can't remember if I came across that way to the client or not. But my only response was, "What do you mean *overcharging* you? In the last three years, I've saved you more than a quarter of a million dollars. Why in blue blazes would you even think I was overcharging you?"

The client replied calmly, "You're overcharging me in commissions, for one thing. My new agent said he could do everything you did and more and he's doing it all for $25,000. I hope you understand, I have to do what's best for my business."

And just like that – BAM! – He was gone!

This actually was my first encounter with this game. I can tell you I didn't like it one bit. In fact, in the pit of my stomach, I knew this was completely wrong. And I had a difficult time accepting it.

As you can probably imagine, I wallowed around for several days in self-pity. God knows, I told myself, I deserved to mourn. I alternatively told myself the agent who "stole" my business from me was either stupid or lying. Sometimes I described him as both. I told myself my client – that is, former client – was making a serious mistake.

But looking back on the entire situation, I realized that these so-called producers have actually discovered a way to win. I also realized that unless I discovered a better way to explain and quantify the impact I was actually having on my clients, I would always be at the mercy of some producer who could do it.

If I didn't change something – and change it quickly – I was standing witness to the agency death spiral that was only spinning ever more quickly out of control.

Who Was Really to Blame Here?

This is exactly when I had another epiphany. My client wasn't to blame. Blaming him would have been an easy way to get over this particular situation. But it wasn't the way to correct it.

The situation, which had just occurred, was my fault. Yes, you heard me right. My fault.

I had wrongly assumed that my client understood the impact we were having on overall costs. I then calculated what percentage of commission the new agent was making. Based on $25,000 divided by $750,000 it was approximately 3.3 percent.

I may have been born at night, but I wasn't born last night. I knew that we were spending more than $25,000 of our own resources on safety and claims management alone.

Had we been able to match the $25,000 fee, we would have only lost money. And yes, at the time, I was very tempted to match it, that's how furious I was.

Now that I look back on it all, this fiasco was without a doubt one of my greatest lessons. Up until this point, I hadn't given much thought about the possibility that as an agency we were contributing to our own demise. We were continuously performing more work and investing more of our own resources in situations like this.

If we couldn't continue to do that year after year, it created a lack of trust that created a chasm larger than the Grand Canyon. They had come to expect us to do more and for them to pay less.

For the first time in my career, I realized I was nothing more than a commodity.

Action Steps

1) Do I win or lose business based solely on the price of the policies I sell?

2) Am I ever in the position in which I'm tempted *not to offer* my clients the best solutions for the for fear I don't get paid or my pay gets reduced?

3) Do I "give away" value added services in order to sell more insurance policies?

4) What do I do if my client wants and needs to protect themselves in other ways than buying an insurance product?

Chapter 9

What The C.R.A.P.? The Professional Agent

"By failing to prepare, you are preparing to fail."
Benjamin Franklin

For all the misgivings and complaints I may have aired about the insurance industry, I still see quite a bit of good. If I didn't, I would never have stayed in it as long as I have.

The beauty of this industry is that each and every one of us is an entrepreneur – or as some would say an "intrepreneur." Being an entrepreneur means that there are no limits to how much we can produce and earn.

Think about what this last statement truly means. No limits on our earnings. That's awesome. For some reason, though, most producers don't seize full control of this fantastic opportunity.

I believe it's due, in part, to the fact that they don't approach their career like a professional. That may sound harsh, but hear me out. In every profession, regardless if its law or sports, the true superstars all put in a tremendous time to prepare and practice their routine.

Could you possibly imagine being an actor and going out on the Broadway stage without going to one rehearsal? Now, that's what I call a high-risk practice. Without those hours spent in rehearsal they would be going on stage practicing, in effect, for the audience. If they messed it up, they certainly won't get another chance at that performance.

Most insurance producers don't do this, though. They use their time in front of their clients as practice – instead of attending rehearsals or hitting the driving range. They're putting on their greens, so to speak, for the first time when they meet their client.

According to the most recent statistics, the industry average for new business production per year is, well, dismal. New producers, according to one report, who have three or less years' experience in the business and/or a book of business less than $300,000, the average new business production amounts to less than $25,000 a year.

And it doesn't get progressively better the more years of business experience an agent has. Those producers with more than three years have books of business that averages between $300,000 to 600,000 and average less than $50,000 in new business each year.

Finally, the report revealed that producers with books of business of greater than $750,000 average approximately $95,000 a year in new business sales.

I now see why less than 40 percent of producers last less than five years.

But there is some good news in all of this dismal talk. These numbers aren't written in stone. These figures don't have to remain static. They can change at any time.

I truly believe that any producer at any time can accomplish anything they desire. All they need to be is dedicated to being purposeful and intentional. They also need to be willing to prepare and practice in a predictable and consistent fashion.

It's that simple. But it certainly isn't easy. You must remember that there are no shortcuts to excelling at your craft. I'm sure you remember the story I told in the previous chapter. The large account I had lost because an agent who beat me by undercutting my fee.

My client believed the other agent when he told him that I had been overcharging him in fees. The truth of the matter is I didn't have a good answer for him. Looking at it now, I have to confess that I wasn't yet a professional. I hadn't practiced enough. It showed. Obviously. I failed miserably in my practicing in front of the client.

Basically, my client fired me. I had failed to be exactly what I was just extolling as the virtues of a professional: intentional and purposeful about my practice time.

Okay, I admit it. I was like nearly every other producer. I rarely practiced or prepared to engage with my clients. I felt I was past that stage. I was a veteran in the business. I knew the business, I knew what I had to do, and quite frankly, I thought I did it well. I truly felt I could get myself out of any tough situation.

I felt not unlike Mohammed Ali, I could float like a butterfly. I could zig and zag my way out of any situation, regardless of how unpleasant it may be. If that didn't work, I thought then the client just didn't "get it." And that wasn't my fault. Or so I thought.

Being "fired" by this client after all the great work we had performed and all the money we had saved him, picked me up by my shirt collar and shook me up pretty well. Yet another epiphany. And yes, I'll repeat it: the entire fiasco was my fault.

I realized after enough time had passed that I could analyze the situation somewhat objectively, that he didn't understand the impact we had on his business, because I failed to properly explain it to him. In fact, I had done a truly horrendous job of laying it all out for him. I hadn't done a good job of quantifying it for him.

After all, it wasn't his responsibility to realize and recognize our role as an agency in his savings – that job landed squarely on my shoulders. I failed to do this. I failed to ensure clarity.

I had to admit to myself that I was playing like an amateur. Had I been performing like a professional I would have been prepared. I would have shown him that we had an impact of greater than $1,000,000 on his company's tier. Should he choose another firm, he was actually jeopardizing that million-dollar impact to "save" $65,000.

The Proverbial Blessing in Disguise

Yes, I realize many individuals say this when they get slammed with some difficult or even devastating situation. But, these events really were a blessing in disguise for me.

I took up the mantle and challenge of nothing less than changing the game. I vowed never to be blindsided like that again.

Several months after this incident had passed; I met with this former client. My goal? To learn from him what I could have done differently.

Initially, his argument remained the same. "I felt it was in my company's best interest to move on to another agency," he said.

While I acknowledged that I understood his needs and respected his wisdom as an entrepreneur, I then explained a few issues I should have told him the first time around.

"Do you realize," I asked him, "that in 'saving' $65,000 you were jeopardizing $1,000,000 or more?" I'll never forget the look on his face. I'm not sure if it was one of anger or embarrassment.

After quite a long pause, he asked what I meant by that. He couldn't understand where I had pulled the million dollar savings from. I offered to run through the details with him quickly.

We spent the next hour doing just that. I reviewed what his situation was when we first started working with him. I reminded him of the tools and resources we put in place for him and his team. Then we discussed his direct and indirect costs associated with his risk-management program.

I even went out on a limb. "I'm sure your profits rose by several hundred thousand dollars," I told him, "every year we were working with you."

Not surprisingly, this last statement interested him. He shook his head slowly and responded, "Yes, they did by the way. But how do you know that. You never saw my financial statements."

I had finally switched gears. Now I was talking like a professional. It felt great to be in a position to speak about something other than his premiums and defending the commission associated with them.

My Journey Toward Professionalism

My quest in becoming a true professional in this business, by the way, wasn't an easy one. But, they say few things really are. First, I had no process to follow. I had to create a process specifically designed for success in the risk management and insurance industries. It was like going on a trip without a map.

As I walked along the path, I took quite a few wrong turns, made my share of mistakes and learned more than I care to admit simply through the process of trial and error. Perhaps the best step I ever took, though, was recognizing that I needed to practice *before* I met with the customer – just like a true professional.

I spent an average of four hours preparing and practicing for every hour I had planned to spend with a client or a prospect. It was amazing. I may have started out wandering in the desert, but I soon began to practice and prepare purposefully.

Before I knew it, I felt quite comfortable with the sales process I created. And it revealed itself in my results. My hit ratio, average size of client and referrals increased significantly.

How I Increased Referrals

You may be surprised to see that, in the process of performing more like a professional, I also increased my referrals. I attacked this systematically. My first step in this was to meet with like-minded professionals in other industries. For example, my three main sources initially were a CPA, a banker, and an attorney. We formed what could only be called a strategic alliance.

One of my strategies in doing this was to meet with these professionals and actually explain my entire sales process with them. In this way, they knew exactly what I would be offering those individuals to whom they referred me.

Several weeks after one of these sessions, I received a call from my CPA ally. He said he had a client that could benefit from our services. The client was working with an out-of-state broker. They felt that no local broker could possibly handle and support their needs. Then he paused for a beat and said, "But . . . "

The word lingered on the phone's air waves in a most ominous fashion. "But, what?" I asked in an attempt to prod the information out of him.

"But, Jerry, I have to warn you. If you're not prepared," he told me straight up, "when you meet with him and his team, you won't last fifteen minutes. They're very direct. They don't want to waste any time. If you can't show them immediately you can manage their account, they'll kick you out in a heartbeat." He took a breath, adding. "Take your "A" team with you. They want the broker to handle all of their risk management needs."

I assured my ally that he wouldn't be embarrassed or regret referring us. We set a meeting time and place. I gave our team a lot of time to prepare. We set our appointment for the following week.

Immediately the following morning I chose a team I knew would prepare and practice. We numbered four all together. First there was my account executive Kris as well as an employee benefits specialist, an investment-retirement specialist and myself.

That day we met for two hours. We discussed our overall strategy and learned as much as we could about their business and this particular project. After that I asked everyone if they felt we were successful in making any headway in being of benefit to the prospect. The answer was a resounding no.

To a person, we all felt if we had to walk up to that prospect at that moment we would fail dismally. We met the following day and practiced and prepared another two hours. How did we do? We all agreed we were making progress, but not nearly prepared enough to meet with success.

The following day we met yet again for two hours. Once we completed this, we felt, as a group, we were 80 percent confident. So we met for a fourth day as well. That's when things really began to mesh. We were confident. We were ready.

Three days after that, we met with the CPA who had referred us, and the prospect. The meeting went very well. We worked as a team and stayed focused on their needs.

Within a week, they hired us and they assigned all of their existing coverage to us. The annualized revenue was greater than $400,000.

The Difference between an Amateur and a Professional

We all learned a valuable lesson with the incident. Purposeful practice and preparation. Amateurs hope to acquire great clients. Professionals know they will acquire great clients – because they've performed whatever leg work it takes to do so.

Now, I'm sure there are more than several of you reading this wondering if the hours we invested in this client were worth our time. Aren't we still merely giving away for free what many call value added services?

Here's how the math turned out.

We were a four-member team. We had four sessions at two hours each. That equals 32 hours. Thirty-two hours of purposeful practice. Divide this by $400,000 revenue we can expect to receive. That comes out to $12,500 per hour per person. Perhaps not such a bad investment of our time and energy after all.

Whatever it Takes!

Now that I look back at my successes throughout my life – whether they were in sports or business – I can see one common thread running through all of them. My success depended on the amount of time I was willing to invest in purposeful preparation. My success depended on the amount of time, in other words, I was prepared to practice.

The more practice and purposeful preparation I invested, the greater my chances were at succeeding.

In fact, if you look at any individual who excels at his specialty, you'll discover that same theme. Take the major league baseball player Tony Gwynn, for example. At the end of 20 years in the major league, he is a hall of famer and ended his career with a .338 lifetime batting average. That, by the way, is one of the best batting averages ever recorded.

He was asked about the secrets to his success. "No secret, really," he replied. He said he merely kept to the fundamentals. Then he explained it a bit further by saying that he had set a goal of hitting 300 baseballs off a tee every day of his career.

Now, most individuals would think that once you reached a certain point in your career you wouldn't have to go through what had to be considered routine and boring practice. Others might be afraid that practicing so much would contribute to a heightened chance of injury.

I am fully confident, though, that Gwynn became one of the best hitters because of his insistence of hitting the ball 300 times daily.

The Very Successful Bo Eason

Bo is one of my business coaches and a friend. I used to describe him as an "overachiever." He said his "Big Dream" was to be the best safety in the world. When he began his college career he was a walk-on. This college walk-on eventually became an NFL first-round draft pick. So how did he do it? You've guessed it: purposeful preparation.

One of Bo's habits was to always be the first player on the field every day -- regardless of what else was happening around him. He did just that in his four years with the Houston Oilers.

In his fifth year of play, Bo was traded to the San Francisco Forty-Niners. Did that change his habits at all? No.

He was determined to be the first one on the practice field with the Forty-Niners as well. The first day of preseason camp he arrived early. Imagine his surprise when he discovered that he wasn't the first – but the second -- player on the field. Who was the first? Legendary Jerry Rice.

They introduced themselves and Bo, being more than a little curious, asked Jerry why he was at practice so early. Jerry's answer was simple. He said he was always the first one there and the last to leave. He had come to practice and prepare. This way, he said, when it was time to play the game, he would be ready for anything!

But the real secret of Rice's success was evident when he practiced with the team as a whole. For those of you who may not have realized it, Jerry Rice is the all-time NFL leader in touchdown passes. Many believe his record will never be broken. As my friend Bo practiced with the defensive backs and safeties, he took notice of how Rice's form of practice differed from the rest of the receivers.

In this particular instance, the quarterback was Joe Montana. He was throwing passes to all the receivers. The receivers were lined up. As their turn came, they would step up to the line of scrimmage. They would run a pass pattern, catch a pass and jog back to the quarterback. Then they would toss the ball back and walk back, get in line and wait for their next pass.

That's not exactly how Rice did it. He sprinted to the line of scrimmage and stood like it was game time. He looked both ways. When the ball is snapped, he sprints a precise pattern, catches the ball and then sprints the entire length down the field into the end zone.

But wait! He's not done yet. Then he sprints back to Montana, hands him the ball and then back in line. Rice didn't do this just once or twice, but for the entire practice time.

When the practice was completed the last two men on the field were Bo and Rice. Bo then asked him why he practiced the way he did. Why run through the end zone every time? After all, no one else did it.

Rice's response speaks volumes about his attitude and intentions. "Bo, that's an easy answer," he explained. "Every time these hands touch the football, I expect to score a touchdown. So, I figured why not train to do just that every time?"

Think about that philosophy for a moment. There's a big difference, when you stop to think about it, in merely showing up to the game trying to catch passes and showing up to the game fully prepared to score touchdowns.

Which one are you doing?

Action Steps

1) How often do you prepare and practice?

2) Do you perform high-risk or low-risk practice?

3) Do you prepare like Jerry Rice or the rest of the pack?

4) Do you want to score touchdowns or are you satisfied with just catching passes?

Chapter 10

The BGRAT System: Balance

Just as your car runs more smoothly and requires less energy to go faster and farther when the wheels are in perfect alignment, you perform better when your thoughts, feelings, emotions, goals and values are in BALANCE."

Brian Tracy

Once my daughter, Kelley, hit me with the question of why I didn't love her, I stood back and took a good objective view of my life. I felt as if I were bearing witness to someone else's life. I felt like I was watching a movie. I also felt a lot like Scrooge, believe it or not.

No, I didn't say "humbug" to the Christmas season. Well, then again, who knows? If you had asked my family, they would probably have answered that question differently.

I felt like Scrooge as the ghosts of Christmas past and future led him through the scenes. There he stood, looking at his life. Basically, you could say he was watching that cliché we all use about our lives flashing before our eyes. His really was.

Granted, I didn't have a ghost lead me to the most grievous errors of my life, but then I really didn't need to. As I revisited my past, I knew after a while where the worst parts of my life lay.

I've got to confess that appointment with my then five-year-old daughter Kelley certainly felt like I was sleepwalking through that day, watching some actor who looked incredibly like me standing in for myself.

To this day, I can point out with amazing accuracy the places in my life where I lost my balance and fell – and as a result failed my family miserably.

Balance? What's Balance?

Before I go any further, perhaps I should explain what balance means in this context. You probably already know. After all if you're a hard-working insurance professional sincerely interested in creating a career, you're probably already grappling with this issue.

I'm not talking about the physical kind of balance. The type in which you steady yourself as you walk or even that type of balance that allows you to ride a bicycle without falling.

I'm talking about being able to walk a tightrope. Okay not a literal one, but definitely, a figurative one. Walking the finely taut, thin rope between your personal and professional lives. It's a conundrum for most of us.

We all take pride in our careers, for any number of reasons. One of the reasons we try to do so well is to help contribute to our family's well being. We want them to have everything they need and, of course, we try to give them as much as what they want additionally. Within reason.

But the kicker is that the harder we work, the less our family gets of the one thing they really want. What's that? You. When push comes to shove, your family can do without many material items, but they can't really do without your presence in their lives.

I learned this lesson the hard way. It's also a lesson that seems to pop up quite often. Every time I think I've learned it, I do something that perfectly illustrates the fact that I don't know it as well as I thought. Then I have to take time to relearn it.

My Greatest Gift

I truly believe that the greatest gift of my life was the fact that I was offered the opportunity to change my workaholic ways before I totally lost my family. I'm hoping that as you read this, it's not too late to save your family life as well, or whatever it is that you love most in life.

It's ironic, isn't it? That we tend to get so involved in our work that we neglect the one aspect of our lives that mean the most to us – our family. I can't tell you how many insurance sales agents I've met who worked hard for their families, only to find that they've grown so far apart they lose them.

The good news is that at any point in your life – and your career – you have the power to change it all. I don't care whether you've been an agent or broker for five or fifty years. At any time along your path, you can successfully initiate changes that make you more responsive to your family's needs.

Perhaps you think the only way to achieve this feat is to curtail much of your work schedule. What if I told you that you can regain control of your family life, while still retaining that lucrative book of business you've dreamed of?

The alternative? Learning it too late in your career only to discover that you've already lost your family. If you haven't lost them due to the legal process of divorce, they may already have removed themselves emotionally from you.

Believe it or not, once you put all the puzzle pieces together, you'll realize how simple the answer is. Notice I said simple. Not easy. If it were easy, I wouldn't have been revisiting the same lessons over . . . and over again.

The Tightrope: Walking the Producer's Walk without Neglecting Family

This is not a new idea. I'm sure that sales agents and producers have encountered this problem since the beginning of time. Balance is vital in your life.

Up until this point in your career, you might have thought that you had to sacrifice one for the other. You may have already chosen – either consciously or unconsciously – one over the other. For many of you, it may have been your careers that have won.

It really doesn't have to be that way, though. If I can repair my personal life and bring my children and wife closer to me, then anyone can. It's never too late to seek to change the way you approach both your work and your family.

I'll be honest with you, even after that fateful playground appointment with my daughter that day; I really didn't learn the lesson as well as I should have. Certainly it was a wake up call, but I still had a lot of learning to do. I knew I had to reclaim my family. I wasn't sure how to go about doing it.

Confusion and Isolation

My initial reaction to the entire scene on the playground that day was one of confusion and isolation. I looked into my daughter's black eyes, as she asked why I didn't love her. Didn't she know that a father's love was unconditional? That I loved her greatly whether we were in the same house or I was at work or if we were enjoying each other's company on the playground.

That's when it clicked with me. Of course, she didn't. She was only a young girl. If my own wife who was, of course, more mature and understanding than a five-year-old was also beginning to doubt my love for her, what could I expect a young girl to think?

But, truthfully, I was hopelessly out of control, isolated and confused. And that was just for starters. What I was feeling was really the reverberations of my worlds clashing. The one world—the insurance producer's world – had just barreled down and hit my other world – my family and personal life – in a head-on collision. And I wanted desperately to leave the scene of the accident.

I knew I could continue to grow my business. But, I also knew that it was going to require putting in an ever-growing amount of time. I didn't mind the time –

because that would ultimately be reflected in a larger bank account.

But try as I might, I couldn't figure out how to make any more hours in the day. We're only given 24 a day. And out of those hours, we really do need to sleep eight of those. That left me 16 hours in my day. One would believe I should have been able to divide my time between work and family . . . obviously I couldn't.

Thankfully I Got to the Bottom of The C.R.A.P.

That may be a strange way to see it, but I finally did analyze the business with enough insight to be able to see The C.R.A.P. As you know, this is my personal acronym for the following attributes:

The – Trust

C   -- Commodity

R   -- Roving targets

A   -- Agency death spiral

P   -- Professionalism

I've discussed these fatal flaws – as I saw them – with you in the previous chapters. I felt lucky to have discovered them. These were the aspects of the business that kept me tied to it, thinking that in order to be more successful, I had to spend more time at work. How wrong I had been.

Hopefully, you'll learn from my lessons and can discover ways that you can spend less time working while making significantly more money.

It surprised me at the time, but looking back it really shouldn't have. With each of the flaws I was able to identify and overcome, I naturally increased the balance in my life.

The Courage to Reduce my Hours

At the beginning of my career journey, I was spending between 60 and 80 or more hours a week focusing solely on my career. As I practiced this new method of working, I was able to reduce my actual working hours during a week to less than 50 and sometimes even as few as 30 hours.

Imagine my delight when I discovered that I could then fill that free time taking advantage of activities with my family. And the timing of my newly learned lessons couldn't have been better. Both Kelley and my son Jared were just starting to play team sports and take part in other activities.

Not only did this allow me to attend all of their games, but it helped me, in an indirect way to reconnect with one of my passions: baseball.

Kelley really wasn't the baseball player. Her activities leaned more toward dancing, gymnastics and swimming. My son, though, loved baseball and soccer as well as basketball and football.

Fortunately, the timing of my life lessons allowed me to coach his baseball teams for nearly 10 years. If I must say, not only did Jared and I – and a core group of young baseball players – thoroughly enjoy ourselves, but we were highly successful.

In the decade or so I coached, I steered them through more than 600 games. Not only that, but at last count, about 20 of these fine players are going on to play college ball. Imagine that!

In addition to helping my children play sports, the time I saved once I understood how to beat those fatal flaws I spent on the golf course. I also spent more time with all aspects of family life and got reconnected with friends I had lost touch with.

The Joy of Taking Family Vacations

We actually took family vacations that consisted more of a quick weekend away, which as you can guess, had been spent for me checking my messages for the entire time I was supposedly vacationing.

The most remarkable aspect of all of this, though, is the amount of time I've been able to spend with only my wife, Lisa, including wonderful getaway trips.

What a glorious feeling! Imagine, if you can, spending all your time at work (that's probably not a stretch for most of you) and then one day have an incredibly large chunk of time open up to spend with those you love -- minus the guilt that you're not out "there" making money.

Now here's the most miraculous aspect of all of this. The more balance I'm able to put in my life, the more and greater opportunities opened up to me.

My life – and especially that of my family – has changed 180 degrees since I've learned the secret of balance. I now realize it's a big, bold world – and it involves so much more than just insurance. Before I learned the truth about the insurance industry I never thought for a moment my life would include all these incredibly enriching experiences.

Today, I can't imagine my life without all these incredibly enriching experiences.

And today, I challenge you to discover experiences that will change your humdrum nine-to-five world, (or 6am to

8pm, like mine once were), into one of wonder and excitement – for both you and your family.

Action Steps

1. Balance is an individual concept. What does balance look like to you?

Don't answer this question quickly or flippantly. Take your time. And whatever you do, don't answer it as if it's an unobtainable goal. Because it isn't.

2. Are you currently experiencing the balance you want and deserve in you life? If not, why not?

3. If you fail to put balance in your life, what would you gain?

4. If you don't practice balance, what are you losing?

Chapter 11

It's Déjà Vu All Over Again: Goals

"If you don't know where you're going, you'll probably end up somewhere else."
Yogi Berra

As humorous as the quote above is, it taught me a very important lesson in my life. I can sum up the lesson in one word: goals.

Don't worry. I plan to expand on this concept. The fact of the matter goals are, without a doubt, the single most important criterion that determines the degree of success you experience in life.

Unfortunately, the concept of setting and reaching goals is exactly what's missing from our lives for the majority of us. Me included. For the longest time I floated through my career without any plans to reach my goals. All I had was a vague notion that I wanted to succeed. But I didn't have a roadmap to get me there.

Yogi Berra, then, definitely had it right: "if you don't know where you're going you'll probably end up somewhere else."

This is not only the "G" in by BGRAT system of success, but it's one of the hardest lessons for us to learn. And I don't mean "us" as in just professionals in the insurance sales industry.

Written Goals: The Visible Difference

Mark McCormack, in his book "What They Don't Teach You in the Harvard Business School," revealed a stunningly surprising statistic. One researcher conducted a study on Harvard students who were enrolled in the MBA program.

He asked the students about their future plans. What exactly did they hope to accomplish and what kind of plans did they have in place to put their plans into action?

Here are the surprising statistics. Only three percent of these Harvard MBA students had written goals and a plan to achieve them. (Remember, we're talking about one of the most prestigious schools in the nation attracting the best students.)

Only 13 percent of the students had formed any goals at all. That left 84 percent of these highly talented and bright students essentially rudderless. They were attending one of the best schools in the nation and didn't have any idea where they were going. You know what Yogi Berra would have said about this, "they were likely to end up someplace else."

"Goals are Dreams that are Taken Seriously"

But that's not the end of the study. Ten years later, the researchers contacted the same students. That 13 percent of students who had goals, but didn't write them down earned, on average, twice what the students did without goals earned. Not too surprising there.

Then there was that three percent that had clearly defined, *written goals and a plan to achieve them.* On average they earned more than 10 times what the other 97 percent of the students did combined!

See, Yogi Berra was right. These students knew where they were going – and got there! In a most stunning fashion.

A Natural Goal Setter

I'm fortunate in this respect. I seem to be a natural goal setter. I thank my parents for playing a large role in this. You see, my parents always encouraged me. They told me I could do anything I wanted to do in life. They never set any limits on what they believed my accomplishments could be. In fact, our whole family was very encouraging in this way. You'll see what I mean by this in a few minutes.

It should come as no surprise to anyone who knows me that my first memory of successful goal setting is when I was 11 years old. And as events turned out, it followed a period in which I had failed to set definite goals. I had just "assumed" my success was secure. We all know what happens when we assume.

As a devoted and darn good 11-year-old baseball player, I found myself sitting in the bleachers watching many of my fellow players participating in the yearly Little League All-Star game. Now, I may not have felt so angry sitting there, except for one thing. I knew I was better, much better, than most of those players out there on the field.

So what was I doing sitting in the stands? In fact, I could clearly see myself among the team playing one of my best games ever during the game.

As each batter warmed up at the on-deck circle, as they walked up to the plate to take their turn at bat, even as they made a play out in the field, I clearly and distinctly saw myself playing right alongside with them.

It was at that very moment that I promised myself that this was the last year I would be in the stands as a spectator. I made a goal that evening. I would always be a member on the Little League All-Star Team. And I was.

Whether my 11-year-old brain knew it then or not, looking back it's abundantly clear to me. The visualization process I used while watching that game fueled my desire and enabled me to work productively toward my goals. As I soon discovered, visualization would become an integral step in any process I created in obtaining my goals.

Déjà vu

You'd think that learning this lesson at such an early age, it would stay with me. I wouldn't have to relearn it. But, surprisingly that just wasn't so. I found myself in a very similar place several years later – and yes, it did involve baseball.

This time I was a freshman in high school. Once again, I found myself sitting in the grandstands watching the varsity team play. Once again I got furious with myself. After all, I knew I was every bit as good as any of those players out there and more than likely, from the way they played, better than most.

As they played this particular game I visualized myself playing right along side with them. Just like I had done several years earlier. I was swinging the bat with them, catching pop up flies, running the bases and sliding into home plate. Nothing, I decided would keep me from playing with that team.

Of course, you can probably guess what happened? Yes! For the next three years of my high school days, I was a member of the team.

Now, I have to tell you at this point that many dynamics probably played into my not initially being chosen to be on the team, not the least of which was my size. I can't blame the coach for overlooking me. I really was small to be playing ball. But that didn't mean I couldn't. That didn't mean I wasn't going to work twice as hard as anyone else to get to play ball.

Many of you may view these two incidents as periods of "failures." But when I think back on them today, they stand out not as "failures" but rather as outstanding learning opportunities. I took what I learned from both of these experiences and applied them to my goal of playing college baseball. I decided to use my ability to visualize playing ball proactively this time, instead of using it as a reactionary tool of something that had gone awry in my life.

Let's just make one thing clear. The reason I was in the stands for both that Little League All-Star Game and my freshman year of high school can be attributed to one thing and one thing only: my waiting for someone else to recognize what to me was clearly an obvious talent. I was waiting for someone to come up to me and tell me what I already knew: I was at least as good as or better than any individual on either of those ball fields.

But I took my learning one level higher as well. If no one recognized it in either of those situations, then I had to make people notice me. It was only by doing that I would be able to take my baseball talent to the next level – the college level.

I Looked at My Liabilities

Quite frankly, my size was a deterrent. I can't blame the coaches for overlooking me. I was only 5 foot six inches tall and I weighed an entire 140 pounds.

So I started on my goal early. During my senior year in high school, I would attend many of the college baseball games in the area. As I sat there in the stands, I would visualize myself in the field with them. I would also tell my friends that the following year they would be able to see me on that field playing with the team.

There was only one snag in the process. Very few coaches were interested in a player my size. I got no offers to play college baseball.

My story could have easily ended there. But, fortunately for me it didn't. My older brother, Larry, believed in my abilities. He agreed with me that I was as good, if not better, than the current crop of college baseball players. When he heard I didn't get a single offer, he encouraged me to become a "walk on." This is a student who simply tries out for the team.

I agreed I would do this. But I also knew that I couldn't wait till the day of the try outs to get noticed by the coaches. Had I counted on this as a strategy, it probably would never happen. I had to do something to make sure that I stood out from all the other walk ons who were vying for the coaches' attention.

I, therefore, made it nearly impossible for the coaches to ignore me. How did I do that? First, two months before the tryouts were scheduled; I started practicing on the field with the returning players. I acted as if I were already one of "them."

But more than just showing up to practice and putting in a minimum of time, I studied the habits of the players. I observed who the hardest-working players were. Then I worked harder than those individuals.

Finally, my day of reckoning came: the moment of try outs. I stood with the returning veterans (How cool is that?). Guess what? Yep, I made the team.

What I didn't know at the time and only learned later in the season, that I wasn't one of the coaches' initial choices. They were going to cut me from making the team. But the returning players I had worked with for the previous two months persuaded them otherwise. They told the coaches I would be a valuable asset to the team.

Because of their kind words and their belief in my abilities, the coaches gave me a chance. That's how I became a four-year starter.

The Lesson Extends Beyond Baseball

The lesson I learned from this extends far beyond the foul lines of the baseball field. I thought about this incident and all the others I encountered in my early years. I clearly recognized one theme running through all of these.

Once I am crystal clear about what I want — about what my goal really is — I'm able to picture or visualize it happening. I saw it so clearly it was like watching a movie of my life. I always achieved my goal and what I had pictured in my mind and held tightly to and played over and over again — well, it always materialized. Without exception.

The only times in my life when I fell short of the marks I set for myself were those instances where I failed to create a concrete plan of action. It was those times when I failed to succeed. In a nutshell, I only failed when I failed at investing the necessary time preparing and practicing. Yes. It really does come down to that. It's that simple.

Since I hit upon that epiphany, I created a sure-fire five step process that guides me to this very day to ensure that I meet my goals.

Dream It!

Believe It!

Prepare and Practice!

Experience it and keep score!

Celebrate and Learn from it!

Notice closely what the second step is, "Believe It." This is vital. Believe it and in yourself even before your goal becomes the reality where others can see it. The hours I spent watching those college baseball games may have just as easily been a waste of time had I not believed that I would be playing on that field in coming years. Yes, ironically, I had to believe it even before it happened. I had to believe it before anyone else did. I had to believe it before I was down there playing ball.

I can guarantee you that if you follow these five steps of visualization and manifestation, you too can achieve any goal you set for yourself and conquer any obstacle that you may be presented with.

I also know from the study I cited at the beginning of this chapter that in all likelihood only about three percent of you are going to take up this challenge.

Are you going to be one of the three percent who get serious, write down their goals and then work through this five-step process? Are you going to be one of the three percent who can potentially earn 10 times more than the other 97 percent in your profession?

Action Steps

1. Realistically speaking, what does your future look like?

2. What are your deepest desires for your professional career and you personal life?

3. Do you have an action plan in place to in order to accomplish your goals and desires?

4. How do you measure your results?

Chapter 12

Relationships and Opportunities

"You can have everything in life if you just help enough other people get what they want."

Zig Ziglar

"People don't care how much you know until they know how much you care."

John Maxwell

"Do unto others as you would have them do unto you."

The Golden Rule

These three quotes contain an abundance of wisdom – they remind us that when you care about others' needs and desires others then care about you. Not only do they care, but they demonstrate that concern through helping you reach your desires and goals.

Sounds simplistic, doesn't it? Too simplistic and perhaps a bit naïve? I can imagine someone out there saying, "Show them even a moment of weakness and they'll stomp all over you." Regardless of what those few naysayers may think, this concept really is a fundamental principle of life.

Did you notice I said *life* and not just the insurance industry? When you learn how to care about others and keep their needs uppermost in your consciousness, you'll discover a transformation in your career – and, indeed, in your personal life.

A wise friend of mine once explained it to me in a way that truly brought it home by using an example from his own negotiating career. He chose to not enter into any type of negotiation unless he was willing to accept the other side of the deal as it stood at the beginning of the process. That meant, even before he began, he had to think long and hard what the other person wanted.

By doing so, he opened himself to a myriad of opportunities that he may have otherwise closed off. Why? Because the individual with whom he was negotiating realized that by taking this stance, he really is looking out for the best interest of all involved – not just his own.

Now, before I go much further I need to stop here a moment to explain that your motivation in all of this really does make a world of difference. If you're only pretending to care about the interests of others or their bottom line, you won't experience very good results. In fact, the chances are excellent that the person with whom you're negotiating will intuitively know.

The Fine Line of Motivation

Ultimately, you need to walk a fine line when it comes to motivation. Your motivation must be sincere, even though, when you do this, you, too, will reap benefits. Don't ever try to manipulate the principle to suit your own needs. That is, don't try to use it out of pure greed.

Not long ago, I found myself in a negotiation, which began to seriously gear up. In the heat of the moment, I suddenly remembered that I needed to consider this very valuable perspective.

I envisioned this deal through the eyes of the other individual. Was I willing to accept what he currently asked for? Merely asking this question had a considerable impact on me. When we initially entered into this negotiation, each side was focused solely on our own separate interests. I couldn't understand how the other side felt. And by how I read the other person's actions, I felt fairly certain he felt the same way. It was abundantly clear we weren't heading in a direction, which would enhance our relationship. In fact, considering the direction in which we were headed, I feared we were about to destroy an otherwise good relationship.

That's when I openly asked the question: Were we willing to take the other side of the deal? Not only did I ask myself that, but I asked him as well. He gave it some sincere thought, but said in the end, he couldn't. "Then, nothing we do right now," I told him, "is going to work out in the long run. It's best that we end the discussion."

Yes, I was willing to walk away from a potential sale because I could not in good consciousness accept his position as he was presenting it. Several days later he called me. "I've given your question a lot of thought," he informed me, "and realized that by looking at the negotiation through your lens is vital to making it work – and work well." We returned to the negotiating table and worked out a deal satisfying and profitable to both of us.

Dan Sullivan, the strategic coach, created four great rules that you can use to guide you through not only creating great relationships, but maintaining them as well. He calls these the Referability Habits. They're really quite simple, and something we should not only all follow, but teach our children. They are:

1. Show up on time.
2. Do what you say.
3. Finish what you start.
4. Say please and thank you.

Just as the three quotes at the beginning of this chapter are simple, these four rules are quite simple. So simple in fact, they need no further explanation. When you read them, that proverbial light bulb probably went off in your head. Isn't this what your parents and teachers taught you?

Of course, it is. But sometimes we deviate from these rules. We all do – without exception. We show up late to meetings. We make promises in the heat of the moment, not thinking much about whether we're able to keep them or not. If some of us really told the truth, we have no intention of keeping these promises. They proved advantageous to us in that critical moment of negotiation. We get sidetracked with other, seemingly more important items, and what we start today gets forgotten tomorrow. Just not enough time in the day, we say in our defense. And heck, who uses please and thank you today anyway?

Can you think of anybody you know who actually follows these rules, anyway? I discovered my life – both personal and professional – transformed completely when I started conscientiously following these rules.

Family First

I started with my family. This probably comes as no surprise to you. I was in the process of trying hard to make amends with them. Especially with my daughter, Kelley. I begin to make a point of telling her what time I would be home for supper – especially as she got older.

If I said I was going to make it to supper with them on a specific evening, I kept my word. I give this as my first example because my family bore the brunt of my not keeping my word, my not showing up on time and not finishing what I started.

Once I started following these four rules with those who meant the most to me, I felt it quite comfortable – yes, even satisfying – to strictly follow the same rules with my clients and colleagues.

Now, carefully survey those individuals you admire most. Can you find some common threads that run through their actions? Examine them a little more closely to see if they follow these four rules? Those who do usually experience the best relationships. Not only that but when something should happen and they have to call because they're late, postpone a deadline because they got sidetracked or anything else, the reactions of others is quite amazing.

They're given a pass, so to speak. "Oh, don't sweat it," they're usually told, "you're normally so on time and good about keeping your word, we can work around this."

These individuals are normally so remarkably reliable that those with whom they're working with know that this is a rare event. They know that something really did occur for them to break their own rules.

On the other hand, an individual who is always running late or fails to follow through and has offered a myriad of excuses is often compared to the boy who cried wolf. After a while, no one really believes him.

In fact, I know some people who I just assume are going to be late for meetings. I kid to close colleagues that these people are living in their own time zones. If a meeting is scheduled for one o'clock, for example, I don't even expect this person to show up until closer to 1:30. Sad, but true. Or I tell them the meeting starts a half hour earlier than it really does.

If you haven't noticed from my comments, these aren't the individuals who I respect as true professionals either. You have to respect me – and being late for a meeting is no way to show respect.

The Referability Habits in Action

Here's a great example of the Referability Habits at work. I had an appointment scheduled for eight in the morning with my doctor. I was asked to get to the office fifteen minutes early in order to fill out some necessary paperwork. So, of course, I did. At 8:15 the nurse ushered me into an exam room – a sure signal that the doctor would be seeing me soon, right? Wrong!

Even though she assured me the doctor would be in shortly, that just wasn't the case. A half hour later, at 8:45, I still hadn't seen the doctor. I asked the nurse where she was. She replied curtly, "I told you she was on her way." Another half hour passed. I asked her again, because the doctor hadn't appeared yet.

Now, it was well after 9:15 – more than an hour past my scheduled time. I waited yet another fifteen minutes and asked again. Yes, you guessed it, I got the same response, "The doctor is on her way." In response, I informed the nurse I was leaving. She seemed taken aback. "You can't leave," she told me, "you have an appointment."

"The doctor is more than an hour and half late," I told her, "I'm leaving. If the doctor wants to see me, she can call me."

The nurse gave me a little snicker. "I doubt that's going to happen," she said, "she's a doctor, you know." The following morning the doctor did call me. "Jerry, I was late because I had a life-and-death emergency with one of my patients. I'm sure you can understand that."

"Of course, I can," I replied. "But if that were the case, why didn't your staff tell me that. I would have gladly rescheduled my appointment. Instead, I sat in your office, being told you were on your way for an hour and half – or more. And all the while they're scolding me because I was impatient." I paused a beat before continuing, "They all acted as if they were doing me a favor by allowing me to be their patient."

In reality, her staff was complacent. They didn't respect my time. They didn't believe that my time was just as valuable as theirs. Much to my doctor's credit, she profusely apologized and apparently had a productive discussion with them. The next time I visited, they all held better attitudes.

It's amazing how much stronger relationships can be created just by following the Referability Habits:

1. Show up on time

2. Do what you say

3. Finish what you start

4. Say please and thank you

When you add these to the basic concept of the Gold Rule and showing others you sincerely care about them, you can't help but find success in both your professional and personal life.

Action Steps

1. Are you consistently on time for your appointments – both professional and personal? Do you do what you've promised and finish what you start? Do you say please and thank you?

2. Do have great relationships in both your personal and professional life? If you do, why? If not, why not?

3. Do your relationships benefit everyone involved or are you the only individual benefiting from them?

Chapter 13

Attitude and Gratitude

"The people who are crazy enough to think that they can change the world are the ones who do."

Steve Jobs

"People who are unable to motivate themselves must be content with mediocrity, no matter how impressive their other talents."

Andrew Carnegie

"If you think you can or think you can't – you are correct."

Henry Ford

"Learn to be thankful for what you already have while you pursue all that you want."

Jim Rohn

"Success is not final; failure is not fatal. It is the courage to continue that counts."

Winston Churchill

"Gratitude is the greatest guarantee of continual, successful interaction with the world over an entire lifetime."

Dan Sullivan

Attitude.

I don't know about you, but the greatest challenge in my life has been – and yes, continues to be – keeping my attitude in check. I've found the secret to my success. As my attitude toward my career and personal life improve and I get more enthusiastic – and I get more thankful for what I already have – my confidence increases by leaps and bounds. Not only that, but as my confidence level increases, I discover I'm more successful.

As you might have guessed, I've also experienced the opposite in my career. As my attitude disintegrates– and I forget to even give thanks for what I already have – my confidence plummets and my performance similarly takes a nosedive.

I've also discovered two truly remarkable facts through the years as well. The first is that, without a doubt, I'm in charge of my attitude. The second came as a surprise to me, but it's true nonetheless. My attitude is also greatly influenced by those individuals with whom I surround myself.

For this reason, I'm careful about who I spend my time with. When I spend time with negative people, those lacking a good attitude and aren't grateful for what they have, I tend to spiral into a similar attitude and it doesn't take long for that to reflect in my performance and my personal life.

You may already know all of this. It took me a while, though, to come to this realization. I was lucky enough as I was growing up to have parents and other family members who supported me one hundred percent. In fact, my parents were not only my biggest cheerleaders, but they were my first life coaches. Of course, I didn't realize it at the time. It was only when I ventured outside the comfort of my family that this became apparent to me.

You might have already realized this. After all, my brother, you'll recall was a strong supporter of my college baseball career. And for that, I'll always be grateful.

My father, additionally, would always tell us children to "plan your work and work your plan." It wasn't until I became an adult that I realized that not everyone was fortunate enough to live in a nurturing environment like me.

The Importance of Gratitude

I normally talk about attitude and gratitude together, because, quite frankly, I love the way the words rhyme. But as someone pointedly told me once, just because something rhymes doesn't make it true. Yes, I have to concede that. But in this instance, there are strong ties between attitude and gratitude.

As part of this early family support, I was exposed to certain ideas. One of the most important concepts I learned was the dichotomy of abundance and scarcity. If you're not familiar with this idea, it's a valuable attitude to be aware of and even a more valuable one to adopt.

In this worldview, there are basically two ways to look at the world. On the one hand you can believe that the world – the economy as well other areas of your life – is based on the concept of scarcity.

In this worldview, individuals truly believe that there are only a limited number of resources – from money to food to even luck if you listen to some people. Some of the characteristics and attitudes of those who operate from the scarcity mentality include:

- Have difficulty sharing recognition
- Find it hard to give credit to others

- Have a hard time being happy for the others

While I've known many individuals who get jealous when another receives a raise, some people actually get depressed when others receive either a raise or some recognition. They're steeped in the scarcity mentality in which they believe that there's a limited amount of economic resources in the world. Unfortunately, much of our society views the world like this – and even our economic system is established according to this belief.

But, there's another way to look at the world – one that you may not have ever been told about. Sometimes, I believe it's been kept a secret because if everyone knew about, then more people would succeed.

I, however, sincerely want you to succeed. I want you to feel the fulfillment of a truly successful life. You need to consider the possibility of changing your worldview to one of abundance. Have you ever met individuals who believe this? Have you noticed similar traits among these persons?

Generally speaking, these individuals have a sense of deep personal worth. They're confident of their own abilities.

The Greatest Difference in These Views

mes down to it, there is one large
en these two worldviews: those with
tality don't care about other people,
hink abundance do care about others.

When viewed from this perspective, the abundance mentality is just an extension of the Golden Rule, which we discussed earlier. You have to sincerely care about others before you can become successful yourself.

And believe me, as you steep yourself in believing that there is more than enough of everything to go around – money, good reliable clients, love, energy, anything you may need – the more successful you'll find yourself. Individuals who adopt the abundance mentality find that more and more of everything flow their way as time goes by. They reap benefits in both their personal and professional life.

If you have not yet discovered this way of thinking, do so today – even for a short time. More money will flow your way. More clients will be knocking on your door. Incredible coincidences will suddenly take place in your life. Try this way of seeing the world from the idea that there's more than enough to go around for one week. That's all – just seven days.

Granted, one week isn't a long time, but if you sincerely set out to do this, you'll discover a noticeable change in your "luck." Go ahead, try it this week. What do you have to lose?

Are You an Abundance Thinker or a Scarcity Thinker?

You'll find that you'll go a lot farther not only in your professional career, but in your personal life as well when you think abundance is the foundation of your world. It's true we all fall back into a scarcity viewpoint at times. When this happens to you, here are four sure-fire suggestions to kick you back into believing that abundance is the true way to believe.

1. Monitor your thoughts

The moment you realize you're falling into a scarcity mentality, stop yourself. Then ask yourself this question: "How is this person's good fortune depriving me of anything?" You'll automatically know the answer: They aren't!

In fact, your next thought should be: that if that person can experience good fortune – you can too. Instead of sulking and feeling jealous, you should be celebrating with him, knowing that your turn is just around the corner.

2. Choose your conversations wisely.

In other words, watch what you're talking about. Don't allow yourself to get dragged into conversations about the things others have – whether they're possessions, great clients or anything else. Instead, ask the other person to talk about his personal and professional accomplishments, then be sincerely pleased for them.

3. Work on your personal growth.

"What?" You say, I work hard enough, let alone spend my off time working on "personal growth."

This may seem like overkill to you initially, but you'll soon discover the wisdom in this advice. You'll find this helps with keeping the abundance mentality uppermost in your mind. What types of personal growth work am I talking about? Activities that build your inherent skills and especially those you enjoy. The goal is to fill your time with finding personal satisfaction so your mind doesn't take you to the dark recesses of what the other person has that you don't.

The goal is that you'll be counting your blessings, giving thanks for all you have, and not thinking that your colleague has more than you.

4. Cultivate new relationships.

Sometimes, we delve deep into a scarcity mentality because those we're keeping company with are entrenched in this way of thinking. If this is the case with you, then it's time you expand your social horizons and find individuals who embrace the abundance mentality. You'll discover it's much easier to stay uplifted and view the world as a wonderful, unlimited place.

The more time you spend working toward a constant, sincere mentality of abundance and plenty, the more you'll find your professional career blooming. Not only that, but you'll discover new, more satisfying levels to your personal life as well.

Are You a Giver or a Taker?

I've found the insurance sales industry can be fairly safely divided into two types of individuals. To be truthful, the population at large can be categorized in this way. You may not have thought of it before. You may not have even considered how you fall into those two categories.

Each day, we all make decisions based on this division. When you make a decision – any decision – that contributes to the welfare of others without considering how you can gain anything from the transaction, you can think of yourself as a giver.

Givers, by the way, usually offer assistance to others in any number of ways. If you find yourself sharing your knowledge of the sales industry with younger, less experienced agents, you're probably already a giver. You may go out of your way to introduce one individual to another who may have a profound influence either in their career or in the personal life. This is another classic sign of a giver.

If, on the other hand, you attempt to get others to perform certain actions based solely on what you need or want, you're a taker. You're taking information, knowledge, even contacts from others without providing them with anything in return.

Much of what we've talked about in this book has brought us to this point. I'm sure you recognize the fact that merely the willingness to help others achieve their goals is the heart of the motivation of any giver. This makes an active, amiable collaboration all the easier. This means it's easier to see your client's needs through their eyes.

All of this may seem easy enough to understand – and right now easy enough to do. But, sad to say, this isn't how the average company – sales and just about every other – is set up.

I've been in many companies and heard about many tales of how sales "contests" are created to pit each salesperson against the other. The results? Two fold, actually. The first is that we're naturally expected to be takers: To start using our resources – and the secrets and resources of others – to come out on top.

Have you ever seen those charts, where each employee is viewed as a jockey riding on a racehorse? As the sales mount each week, the images of these contestants are moved a bit farther along the "race track" to the finish line.

The second result is that we are asked to believe that there is only a limited amount of resources. We're invited – even encouraged – to believe that the world is based on scarcity. The faster I race toward the finish line, the more I get and that means there's less for you when you finally do reach it.

Attitude and Gratitude Revisited

Now you have at least an inkling of an idea why I believe that – despite the fact the words rhyme – attitude and gratitude go hand in hand in nurturing your success in the sales industry – in any business venture, for that matter.

I want to leave you with two final ideas. One of these I've gleaned from studying the writings of Strategic Coach Dan Sullivan, the other culled from my own actions. Sullivan insists that you need to make only two decisions to turn your career around if you're feeling as if you're flailing through your days.

The first is to rely solely on your own skills and abilities when it comes to your own professional viability. Don't live off the coattails of another person – not your father, your mentor or even some iconic hero you've looked up to. You'll find an immense satisfaction when you do this.

Secondly, don't feel as if you're entitled to anything – anything at all. Because you're not. Until and unless you first provide value for others, don't expect anything in return. Being a taker does not guarantee your success.

Insurance sales isn't about accumulating leads, clients and piles of money. Oh, you may have had the impression when you walked into it that's what happens. You'll certainly be successful for a short time, even if you do hold these views. And you may be able to make a fantastically successful living.

But sometime, somewhere, you'll reach the point where the hours you invest are not worth the income you're receiving. You'll find that your mentality of scarcity will surface in the glaring fact that there aren't enough hours in the day to earn any more money than you already have – even though your supervisors may be breathing down your back to do even more.

I started this chapter with quotes about attitude and gratitude. Having them in front of me on a daily basis really helps me stay focused on the positive and about what I can achieve rather than what I can't!

There is a poster hanging on my wall. It's of an eagle flying high that says EXCELLENCE "Excellence is the result of caring more than others think is wise; risking more than others think is safe. Dreaming more than others think is practical and expecting more than others think is possible"

Over the past 10 years, I've coached more than 600 baseball games with 20+ teams. Two teams in particular that stand out to me were certainly not the most talented, but they had the best attitudes. The first team was comprised of 11 year olds. Most of the time we were competing against teams of 12 year old boys. These boys loved to compete and weren't afraid to compete. This particular team was small in size but big in heart. Every tournament we played in, we were questioned whether we were old enough or if we were placed in the wrong bracket. The fun part was beating most of those teams. This team played so well together that they won enough tournaments to qualify for the USSSA World Series. We were one of 64 teams from throughout the country to qualify. Our first game in the tournament was against a really good team from Dallas. I'll never forget the warm-up for this game. I overhead one of their coaches saying "Let's get this game over quickly - can you believe how small those boys are?" How could they have ever qualified for this tournament?" Then I see their players pointing over at our boys and laughing as if they thought the game was already over. They would soon find out that it wouldn't be long before the game was over - just not the way they thought it would end.

We played flawless. We had a saying with these boys. It was "make the routine, play routine". We did and we beat this team 21-7. After the game one of their coaches came up to me and said "Coach, I'm not sure how you just did that to us, we're obviously much bigger, faster and more talented than your boys, yet you just killed us". I have to admit, I really wanted to rub it in his face, but that would have taken away from the boys victory, so instead my response was, "Yes, these boys are small, but they have such a great attitude and just go out and play the game the right way every day. Because of that they can't help but be successful."

The other team that will remain a favorite of mine was similar to those I just described, as they were mainly runts that loved to play the game. They all showed up to practice on time and did everything we asked of them. This team was comprised of eight 13-year-olds and four 14-year-olds. We competed in a league where most of the kids were 14. The story is very similar, and our success was too! This team won their League, then District, and then State Championships. We won every close game, because they believed they could and they were also confident because they put in the time in practice.

Now I'm coaching Producers. The results are the same. The ones with great attitudes who want to learn and are willing to work at it are excelling. I'm positive that a person's attitude has a lot more to do with their success than just raw pure talent.

Gratitude List

The second idea comes from my own personal actions. If you recall, at the beginning of this chapter, I explained how my own attitude of thankfulness paralleled my success – financial and personal. Because of this connection, I sit down on occasion and write out a list of ten individuals who I'm very thankful to have in my life.

There's nothing new in this advice. Many persons are already keeping gratitude journals. But, I've taken this one step farther. I mail these individuals handwritten thank you letters, telling them how grateful I am that they're in my life and how they've made me a better person.

I make sure these are handwritten and not just typed hastily on my email account with a quick hit of the send button. I give a lot of thought to this list. Sometimes they include people who I've drifted away from. Some of these individuals I no longer see on a regular basis, but still feel the impact of their teaching, love, kindness and generosity daily.

Some of these persons are relatives or current colleagues. In either case, the time is well spent. While I don't expect any type of response, I typically get wonderfully favorable responses. Imagine how you would feel, for example, if someone you knew long ago sent you a letter telling you how you changed his life.

If you've never done this, sit down and at least write a gratitude list of ten individuals today. Better yet, let these individuals know how thankful you are while you still have the chance.

Action Steps

1. What is your perspective of the world (and be honest!): one of scarcity where it's really a dog-eat-dog world or one of abundance in which there's more than enough of everything to go around?

2. If you can't see or feel the abundance yet, what are the first steps you can take to transform your worldview?

3. From what you've learned in this chapter, are you a giver or a taker? If you're not a giver, what steps can you take right now to become a giver?

4. Write down the names of 10 individuals who have unselfishly given of themselves to help you – either in your professional career or your personal life. Now, write them a letter (emails don't count) telling them how much you appreciate them and how they help make you a better person.

Chapter 14

Tools, Coaches and Mentors, Oh My!

The Essentials

"Great coaches see more in you than you can see in yourself."

Bo Eason

A carpenter would never go to work without his hammer and nails. A writer would never sit down to work on his trade without a computer or paper and pen. And an artist takes brush and paint firmly in grasp before starting her day.

So what makes you think you can trot off to work everyone morning, leaving some of your most important tools at home? Do you even know what your most important tools are?

Most of us haven't a clue what our most effective, efficient, and productive tools are. But, just like those three examples I just gave, you can be sure that, indeed, you do have tools with which you work on a daily basis. Not only that, I'm betting that either in your office or at home, you have even more tools that you may not use every day, but you own because you know that periodically you'll reach for them.

Three Categories of Tools

Personally, I break my tools down into three separate categories. The first, of course, are those I use every day. I like to refer to these as the ones I store in my "tool belt." Just like the carpenter I mentioned earlier, I place these figuratively in a belt I wear around my waist. These tools are within easy reach. Wherever the day should take me I'm sure to have them with me – because they're strapped around me – just like a carpenter's tool belt.

The second set of tools I ensure I have at my disposal are kept in what I like to call my tool box. These are the tools I use weekly. They don't need to be within an arm's reach every day, but I need to be able to access them quickly on a weekly basis.

My third set of tools, I only use on a quarterly basis – once every couple of months. These don't need to be stored very close at all — not even as close as I store those in the tool box, but they need to be kept together. This means when I do need them, I don't have to swear while I spend half a day finding them. Proper storage also means that when I do pull them out of the shed, they're in good condition.

While knowing where each tool is stored at any given time is important, it's even more important to understand what your tools are. This means you need to know the number of tools you have at any given moment. While you may think you already know that intuitively, stop to think right now about your most effective effective tools.

Think about your tools. Can you identify them using this or a similar system that works for you? Do you know how often you use a particular tool? And do you know where they're stored right this moment? If you don't, then it seems as if you have an organizing adventure ahead of you. Before you go much further in you quest for success, you may want to sit down and make three lists: one of the tools that fill your tool belt, one that comprises those implements in your box and the third of everything you use from your shed. Now, you're ready to go forward with your day and your career.

Does Your List of Tools Include Coaches and Mentors?

In a previous chapter, we talked about habits of the best performers in the world, whether it was in the realm of sports, music, acting or any other profession. The one common denominator that ran through their lives was the fact that every one of them had a coach.

And think about it. No Olympic athlete ever gets that far without a coach. The best vocalists in the world have voice coaches. Even your son or daughter playing soccer has a coach who helps him or her improve. What makes us think that we can get to the top of our game without the use of a coach?

I also told you that for the first two decades of my career, I tried to work and practice my trade without the aid of a coach. I had a host of excuses starting with "That was just out of my budget, I just couldn't afford one." The truth of the matter, looking back at my situation now, was that I couldn't afford not to have one. Hindsight is truly 20/20.

It took me a long time to wake up to this fact even though the facts were practically screaming at me. I would discuss the matter of coaches with my colleagues – all of them more successful than me. And, by the way, all of them had . . . yes, you guessed it . . . coaches.

Not only that they had coaches but, not a single one of these colleagues were shy about telling me they owed their success to . . . their coaches. Still I didn't pick up on the hint.

As you recall, I had said my thinking in this area was completely backwards. As I begin to seriously reflect on matters, I realized that any time I had great success in anything, I did have a great coach standing beside me. In fact, I've tried hard to think of a time when I had a great coach and my performance didn't improve exponentially.

One of my coaches who I've mentioned briefly in a previous chapter was Bo Eason. He explained why this is practically a law. "Great coaches see things in people that they can't see in themselves." Hmm. How true. The coaches are able to hold that vision of us that we sometimes can't (or won't) see.

Looking back on my professional career, if I were able to start over, I would change the way I did several things. First, I would make good use of a coach from my very first day on the job. Actually, I do believe I would go one step further. I would find a great coach for every skill at which I wanted to excel.

A few of my favorite tools are:

Kolbe - www.kolbe.com
Assessment for **how** you take action

Strengths Finder - www.strengthsfinder.com
Discover your top 5 talents

Standout - www.standout.tmbc.com
Strength assessment that reveals the personal edge that will help you at work

SPQ Gold - www.salesassessmenttesting.com
Sales assessment test

Win180 Producer Growth Program – www.elevation180.com
Workshops for Producers who want to grow their new business sales bigger, faster, and easier

What Else Would I Change?

I would become a member of those three percent of the population that create written goals. Then I would pay attention to them. Had I done this, I'm certain I would not have found myself wandering in the wilderness, estranged from my family and friends. I'm sure that had I written goals I wouldn't have spent sixty plus hours a week in order to call myself successful.

The other change I would make would have been to make a more productive use of the mentors I had in my life – and probably seek out even more. I mentioned in a chapter that I was privileged in my life to have a few mentors – my dad and my brother, for example.

At the time I don't think I realized just how they influenced my life. At the time, it didn't even occur to me to call them mentors. Looking back now, I realize how fortunate I was to have them there. They not only helped me to fully develop my talents, but they believed in me when I wasn't even sure I believed in myself.

If you don't at least have a mentor in your life right now, I urge you to find one. This should be an individual who you admire – someone who "has been there, done that" as they say and has done it well.

Don't be shy about asking him or her. I can virtually guarantee you that person you ask will be flattered and pleased to accept the position. I was told this many times before I finally gained the courage to ask someone. They, no doubt, will recall all those instances in their lives when they sought help and received it. They are, no doubt, the givers of your profession. Those who sincerely want to see those around them excel and prosper. When I finally did ask someone, they were – yes, you know how this sentence ends – pleased, flattered, and willing.

Do It Now!

The key to your success is to gather your tools, coaches and mentors around you as early in your career as you can. Don't wait – like I did – nearly two decades before you realize the importance of these. Those three factors, plus a concise, yet detailed, set of goals will help you fulfill your wildest dreams – both in your professional and personal lives.

And the best part of that, you won't have to hear your children ask you, like, my daughter, Kelley asked me, "Why don't you love me, Daddy?" If you can't bring yourself to gather these implements around you for your own benefit, do so for the love of your life!

Action Steps

1. What are the tools you need to perform your job well? List the tools you carry daily in your "tool belt," as well as the ones you use weekly that you store in your tool box and those you use only monthly or quarterly and are stashed in your "tool shed." Take your time with these lists. Make sure you include all of your tools.

2. Do you have a coach? If not, list all the reasons (excuses?) you continue to recite why you don't. Then,

list all the reasons why you would benefit from the services of a coach. You know the next logical step to take.

3. Are you one of those three percent of individuals who have written goals? If not, sit down and think of what your goals really are. If you can't think of anything specific, it's time to give this area of your life some serious thought. It may take a while, but, make a list. You'll discover that the mere act of making a list will make you more aware of the course you're currently traveling.

4. How many mentors have you had in your life? Can you call any of family member's mentors as you were growing up? If you can write their names down and in a word or two, describe how they helped you.

5. Do you have any mentors in your professional life right now? If you don't, why not? Can you think of at least one individual you know whom you admire? Would this person be willing to act as your mentor? You never know until you ask!

Conclusion

I hope, as you've read along, you've already begun to use these principles in your life. Let's face it, the sooner you get started on incorporating them into your professional and personal lives, the quicker they'll become a part of you.

When you learn how to allow these principles work through you, without any thought that they are actually changing you, that's when you'll experience your best results. You'll find that with each successful step you take, you'll become emboldened, encouraged and energize to pull these weapons out of your arsenal and take aim against mediocrity.

You'll discover that between overcoming the five fatal flaws — The C.R.A.P. -- and enlisting the nearly miraculous powers of the B.G.R.A.T. System, you'll find yourself, working less and enjoying it more.

Not only that, but the combination of putting these two components of excellence to work really will seem like a miracle. You'll be spending more time with your family. That, in itself, is worth its weight in gold.

Don't be shy about telling others about this incredible system. But whatever you do, don't ever forget how the consistent, persistent use of these ideas and concepts has accelerated your power to earn. Don't ever take for granted what these ten components of a successful career can really do for you. All you have to do is put them to use. I'm betting, if you already haven't done it, you'll soon be posting these on your wall, as a constant reminder of how they've improved your life.

I would be remiss to tell you that one of the most spectacular parts of this plan is that of finding a great coach. You may believe you can't afford one. But, give it the serious thought it deserves before you dismiss it. Don't do like I did. Ignore the writing on the wall for so long.

Looking back at the times when I have been the most successful, the common theme was that I always had a great coach. Early in my career, I had the misconception that I couldn't afford a coach or I didn't have the time to utilize one. I now strongly believe that the fastest way to mastery of anything involves a great coach. My only caution to you is to give this serious thought. The coaches that are the best are the ones that have actually walked in your shoes. There are a lot of theorists out there who proclaim to know what they're talking about. I prefer to work with coaches who have actually done it at a very high level. Go for the Pros and I promise you your results will come bigger, faster and easier!

My newest Dream is to transform the insurance industry, by having a billion dollar impact on new business growth. It's going to happen by coaching producers who want to grow and are willing to work it!

As I've written this book, it's reinforced how each of the 5 fatal flaws and the 5 fortune filters intertwine and connect. They each have an impact on the other. The Win180 Producer Success Program was built with each of these in mind. I've simplified my 30 years of experience as a producer and agency owner to create a system to help others eliminate the pain I felt when my daughter Kelley asked me why I didn't love her, and to be able to achieve the same results I was able to accomplish after I created a different way.

I believe in finding a better way and sharing it! I accomplish this by helping producers to create more value, make more money and free up their time. I'd love to talk with you to discuss how to help you create a unique advantage to dominate your market and to Win on Purpose!

A few People can self-implement, but most people only meet their full potential with the right coach showing them the way. So if you were nodding your head in agreement while reading this book, then it's time for you to take action! Go to our website at: www.elevation180.com and provide us your contact information in the "Contact Us" area. We will reach back out to you and set up a phone call with you to see where your future is going and determine how we can support you in accelerating your success!

Remember, following these tenets of success will totally change the way you look at both your career and your personal life. But more than that, your family will be grateful, because they'll finally have you back in the house – and at the playground or at the soccer or baseball field. Right where you belong.

By the way, that five-year-old, Kelley, is now 21 and in her senior year of college and doing awesome! Jared, who was only 2 at the time, is a senior in high-school and helped lead his team to last year's state high school baseball championship. And Lisa, the love of my life, and I will be celebrating our 26th wedding anniversary and will soon be empty nesters. I'm so grateful that I was there with them and didn't miss it!